First Published on Amazon Kindle Direct Publishing in Great Britain in 2024.

Cover Image & Royal Navy Logo Copyright © Ministry of Defence - Royal Navy, 2023.

Complete Content Copyright © Antony Simpson, 2023-2024.

The right of Antony Simpson to be identified as the Author of the Work has been asserted by them in accordance with the Copyright, Designs and Patents Act 1988.

All rights reserved. No part of this publication may be reproduced, stored in a retrieval system, or transmitted, in any form or by any means without the prior written consent of the author, nor be otherwise circulated in any form or binding or cover other than that in which it is published and without a similar condition being imposed on the subsequent purchaser.

Antony Simpson's Website/Personal Blog: www.antonysimpson.com

Version 1.3

Other Books By The Author

The Alcohol Therapy Workbook
This workbook has been designed for anyone that is struggling with alcohol or has struggled with alcohol in the past.

It is written in a Motivational Interviewing style, one of the key therapies used to support people with alcohol issues. It has been designed using a trauma-informed approach and is strength-based.

What you will find in this book is more than just worksheets about alcohol. You'll find all the tools someone needs to get into recovery from alcohol and stay there. It's a therapy-based book, not an alcohol-based book.

SpellCast - Folk Magic for the 21st Century (co-authored with Luna Hare)
SpellCast is a comprehensive compendium of spells, oils, charms and talismans. It is purely a book about magic, folk magic for the 21st century. The spells are ones that are tried and tested, with some that will stand the test of time.

In SpellCast you will read about the power of Instant Magic, of Banishment & Bindings, Blessings, Cleansing, Communication, Death, Employment, Finance & Money, Fertility, Friendship, Happiness & Joy, Health, Love & Relationships, Luck Magic, Protection, Transformative Magic and WishCraft. This book will change your life. Your life will be abundant in all meanings of the word.

Mental Health Wison - Developing Understand & Empathy
This book contains everything that you need to know about mental health and mental illness.

Mental Health Wisdom is divided into three sections.

Understanding is section one and is all about the facts of mental health.

In section two, Empathy Through Lived Experience, the author shares his personal experience of mental illness.

Life Hacks is section three. It's all about self-care and quick and easy ways to improve your mental health, prevent mental illness or relapse of mental illness.

All available to buy in various formats internationally on Amazon.

This book is dedicated to all those who serve in the Armed Forces and their Family & Friends. Thank you for the work you do around the world to keep us safe and in serving us.

My thanks also goes to our Veterans and their Family & Friends.

It is dedicated to Roy, my Royal Navy Friend. I couldn't be prouder of you. Thank you for being my dear friend and for allowing me to share some of the content of the emails I've sent to you.

My final dedication is to you - the reader. Thank you for buying this book. I hope you enjoy reading it as much as I enjoyed writing it.

Contents

Week	Title	Page(s)
	Introduction	8-9
1	10 Dinosaur Facts	10-11
2	Some Wonders of the World	12-14
3	Navy Jokes	15-16
4	Inspirational Quotes	17-18
5	Weird UK Laws	19-20
6	Would You Rather?	21-23
7	Most Common Myths	24-26
8	Gay Animals	27-30
9	A List of Qualities in People that Inspire Me	31-32
10	Future Technology to Be Excited About	33-35
11	25 Date Ideas	36-37
12	How to Fight a Shark	38-39
13	How to Woo a Turtle	40
14	Some of the Most Amazing Jobs in the World	41
15	The Cycle of Change	42-43
16	Things To Look Forward To	44
17	Facts About Castles	45-46
18	Dad Jokes	47-49
19	Do Aliens Exist?	50-51

20	Solve These Puzzles	52-53
21	The Best-Selling Objects of All Time	54-57
22	Some of the Most Impressive Inventions by Mankind	58-59
23	Facts About Disney that You Probably Didn't Know	60-61
24	The Kindest Humans	62-64
25	A List of Cakes	65-67
26	Dark Jokes	68-69
27	Why Do People Hoard?	70-71
28	Tips to Deal with Loss	72-74
29	What To Do if You Meet a Dolphin	75-76
30	Manners	77-78
31	13 Weird Body Facts	79-80
32	Bottom Humour	81
33	10 Ways to Be More Creative	82-83
34	Stress: What It Is & How To Beat It	84-85
35	Will AI Robots Take Over The World?	86
36	20 Super Space Facts	87-89
37	Bar Jokes	90-91
38	Famous Film Quotes	92-93
39	9 Travel Tips	94
40	Ancient Egyptian Curses	95-96

41	Things Money Can't Buy	97-98
42	Whatever Happened to The Roman Empire?	99-100
43	Mood Lifters	101
44	Neurodiversity Super Powers	102-104
45	10 Weird Olympic Games	105-106
46	Some Wonderful Words We Should Use More	107
47	How to Teach a Sea Lion to Dance	108-109
48	The Great Emu War of 1932	110-111
49	Quiz: Flags of the World	112-113
50	Legendary Characters from the UK	114-115
51	A Survival Guide to a Zombie Apocalypse	116-117
52	Ida & Louise Cook: An Extraordinary & Inspirational Story	118-120
	Afterword	121

Introduction

I remember when my close friend Roy told me about his lifelong dream to join the Royal Navy. Of his desire to protect and serve.

I've called my friend Roy throughout this book to protect his anonymity, career and potentially his safety.

Roy told me of growing up listening to stories of his Uncle's time and Grandad's time in the Royal Navy. I had never seen Roy's eyes as brightly lit and him as animated as he was that day.

I remember saying: So what's stopping you from doing it?

Roy had all sorts of worries. He worried about not being the youngest recruit and that he needed to improve his fitness.

Knowing that Roy had already thought this idea through thoroughly, I said something like: So, how are you going to do it?

Roy proceeded to tell me his detailed plan. I have never seen anyone want something so much. I encouraged him and supported him in this endeavour, through the highs and the lows. The determination, commitment and hard work all paid off with an offer of a place on basic training.

I had mixed feelings about Roy going away for his basic training. On the one hand, I was (and continue to be) incredibly proud of him. On the other hand, there was a sense of loss, I had grown used to his presence in my life and we communicated frequently. I knew things would change.

But I wanted to continue to support, entertain, make laugh and maintain my bond with Roy. So I came up with the suggestion of sending him a weekly email on random topics. The topics I promised would always be entertaining, sometimes interesting, sometimes funny and occasionally serious.

Basic training in the Royal Navy is 10 weeks long. But knowing that Roy would likely be deployed in a different part of the country or world once he passed out, and because I got carried away - I wrote 52 weekly emails to him.

This book contains these electronic letters to Roy.

My Royal Navy Friend

I have chosen to remove some of the more personal information from these exchanges, but the main body of the content is here.

I have no idea what it's like to be in the Armed Forces. But I imagine it's like life in general, filled with ups and downs. I hoped that these emails would help to maintain our friendship. I hoped they served as reminders that I am still here, still in his corner and still (and always) incredibly proud of him.

I miss Roy at times, but know that he is happy, off living his lifetime dream onboard a ship somewhere.

I have absolutely no problem with you using this idea of sending weekly emails to your partner, friend or relative serving in the Armed Forces. I think they would probably love it. So after you've read this book, get started on your first email to your loved one.

Now, on to the emails -

Royal Navy Facts & Stories:

Dispersed throughout this book are Royal Navy facts and stories. These facts and stories weren't sent in my emails to my friend Roy. Mainly because he most probably already knows them.

But I thought the reader might find them as fascinating as I did when doing research and learning about them.

Week 1 - 10 Dinosaur Facts
Hello Roy!

Welcome to the first of your weekly emails. I hope your first week of basic training has gone smoothly Grandpa.

It is well established between us that I love dinosaurs and that there's always a dinosaur involved in every conversation. So this week's email is all about dinosaurs. Here are some interesting facts:

1. Chickens and other birds are all descended from dinosaurs.

2. More than 900 different types of dinosaurs existed, my favourite is always gonna be the Velociraptor because of their ability to open doors in Jurassic Park.

3. Some dinosaurs actually had fur and feathers, rather than the scales we tend to think of them having.

4. Dinosaurs can be carnivores, herbivores or not fussy (i.e. will eat anything).

5. For a long time, baby dinosaur fossils were thought to be different species to their adult counterparts. Then some bright spark sussed out that the smaller fossils were actually babies/younger dinosaurs of the same species.

6. Many people believe that an asteroid from outer space crashed on the planet's surface killing the land-based dinosaurs. There was indeed an asteroid that crashed near Mexico around the time the dinosaurs died off, but other theories include: climate change or the poles shifting.

   Oh there's also a fascinating theory about outer space shape-shifting lizards, but don't get me started on that one.

7. I can't find any evidence that the dinosaurs in Jurassic Park were paid fairly or had employment rights. I'm also unsure as to where these dinosaurs came from!

8. The awful creatures known today as crocodiles share some ancestry with some dinosaurs.

9. A T-Rex can't make a bed, because its arms are too short.

10. We don't know for definite what colours dinosaurs were. So by this reasoning a pink, sparkly glittery one could have existed. Being the campest dinosaur in history.

I hope these facts were entertaining and made you smile. I look forward to writing to you next week.

Best Wishes,

Antony

Royal Navy Fact:

The Royal Navy's longest ever campaign was to stop the transatlantic trade of slaves. This campaign started in 1807 after the Act for the Abolition of the Slave Trade.

Week 2 - Some Wonders of the World
Hi Roy,

I hope that this week, life is treating you well and that you're enjoying yourself (don't be dirty!). Know that I'm extremely proud of you and that you've got this.

Part of the reason you've joined the Royal Navy is to travel the world. So this week I thought I'd tell you about some Wonders of the World.

StoneHenge, UK - It's an eerie place to visit. I've been, see photo below. It's a prehistoric monument that even today, we're not sure how it was made or why. There are plenty of theories of course. It's actually a series of stone circles, rather than just one. Weirdly, there's also a Woodhenge nearby and the beautiful Avebury stone circles.

It's worth a visit, although English Heritage won't actually let you get close to the stones. Oh and be sure to take snacks for the crows that travel from miles around to feast off the food that the tourists bring.

The Pyramids, Egypt - I would love to see the pyramids and ancient sites of Egypt. My brother once went and brought me back a small rock, which was part of the Great Pyramid. But shh, don't tell anyone as apparently taking part of the pyramid is frowned upon.

What has stopped me from visiting Egypt is the descriptions I've heard of security staff on the tourist coach excursions having to carry guns to protect the tourists from the locals.

Chichén Itzá, Mexico - Is an ancient city that was built by the Mayan people. Not just architecturally beautiful, I believe that understanding more about the Mayans is key to unlocking the true history of humanity as a species. A place I would love to visit and learn more about.

Machu Picchu, Peru - Is set on a mountain ridge and was built by Incans. I would love to visit it for the same reasons I'd love to visit Chichén Itzá.

Colosseum, Italy - The Roman Empire has always fascinated me since I learned about it in school. The Colosseum was an entertainment venue, where Roman citizens would go to see gladiators fight in the arena, usually until one of them lay dead.

Taj Mahal, India - India is a massive and incredibly beautiful land. If money and time were no object, I would spend years exploring its wonders.

Some years ago when my friend Robert went to India to marry an Indian woman named Neha, I was lucky enough to be invited to share their celebrations.

Whilst in India I got the opportunity to visit the Taj Mahal, Agra Fort, India Gate and Gandhi's Grave.

The Taj Mahal is symbolic of love. It is a white marble tomb designed and built for an Emperor's deceased wife. The four towers in the corners are actually built at an angle, so wherever you view them from they appear perfectly straight.

The Emperor had plans to build an identical building across the riverbank, but in black marble as a tomb for himself. However this was never completed.

Here is a photo of me at the Taj Mahal:

Hadrian's Wall, UK - Okay, so Hadrian's Wall isn't a wonder of the world. But I reckon it should be. It was a 73 mile wall from one side of the North of England to the other. Built by the Romans to keep the barbarian Scottish people from stealing their land, animals, treasures and people for slaves.

Hadrian's Wall stood at 8-12 feet tall, with varying degrees of width. Along the wall are forts, milecastles and turrets. It is estimated that around 10,000 soldiers (including horsemen) were stationed on Hardian's Wall.

The Romans eventually abandoned the wall. It is rumoured that in some places locals on both sides of the wall deconstructed it to make other structures, such as homes, public buildings, etc.

Here is a photo of me at one of the better preserved parts of Hardian's Wall:

Well, I've rambled on enough for this week. Until next week.
Big Hugs,
Antony

Week 3 - Navy Jokes

Hi Roy,

I thought I'd lighten your mood this week and hopefully make you laugh. I have rummaged around the internet looking for the funniest navy jokes I could find. So although I can't take credit for any of these jokes, I do hope that they have the desired effect.

1. In the Navy Recruitment office, the Recruiter asks: "Do you know how to swim?"
   The guy answers: "Why have you run out of ships?"

2. Why do they prefer non-swimmers in the navy? They defend the ship with much more enthusiasm.

3. How does a Captain convince his crew to stop peeing off the back of the ship? He gives them a stern talking too.

4. What do you call a Navy Officer with a prolapsed rectum? Bad ass.

5. Why is pirating so addictive? Because they say that when you lose your first hand you're hooked.

6. What does N.A.V.Y stand for? Never Again Volunteer Yourself.

7. How did Viking sailors communicate? They used Norse code.

8. What is a sailor's least favourite vegetable? A leek.

9. How do retired Navy Officers greet one another? Long time no sea.

10. I had a dream that the ocean was orange. It was Fanta sea.

11. I was trying to make up a joke about the ocean. But I couldn't think of anything Pacific.

12. What did one sailor say to the other when they had a problem? See we are in the same boat.

13. What do sea monsters love to eat? Fish and ships.

14. What do sailors use to blow their noses? Anchor-chiefs.

15. The navy is starting to recruit blind people. Apparently they're sending them out to sea.

16. What's a sailor's favourite type of film? A sea-quel.

That's it for this week. I hope the basic training continues to go well. I miss you, but imagine that you are loving every second of it.

Until Next Time,

Antony

Royal Navy Fact:

In 1802, Matthew Flinders was the first to circumvent Australia. He was also the first to name the new land mass as Australia in one of his maps.

Week 4 - Inspirational Quotes

Hello My Friend,

This week I'm hoping to inspire you with some quotes, so here goes:

"All our dreams can come true, if we have the courage to pursue them." - Walt Disney

"Do what you can, with what you have, where you are." - Theodore Roosevelt

"Success is not final, failure is not fatal: it is the courage to continue that counts." - Winston Churchill

"Try not to become a man of success, but rather become a man of value." - Albert Einstein

"Happiness is not something ready made. It comes from your own actions." - Dalai Lama

"How wonderful it is that nobody need wait a single moment before starting to improve the world." - Anne Frank

"A winner is a dreamer who never gives up." - Nelson Mandela

"You define your own life. Don't let other people write your script." - Oprah Winfrey

"I have not failed. I've just found 10,000 ways that won't work." - Thomas Edison

"How to stop time: kiss. How to travel in time: read. How to escape time: music. How to feel time: write. How to release time: breathe." - Matt Haig

"Be yourself. Everyone else is already taken." - Oscar Wilde

"It is often the small steps, not the giant leaps, that bring about the most lasting change." - Queen Elizabeth II

"Attitude is the 'little' thing that makes a big difference." - Winston Churchill

And finally two quotes from yours truly. The first is a funny one and the second - something I believe with my whole heart:
1. I had a near-death experience the other day, my whole life flashed before my eyes and I thought: Wow, that's a good amount of napping.

2. Never regret anything that you do or don't do. Be authentic. Remember that with every decision or indecision there is an opportunity to grow, learn and develop. And above all, be happy.

Best Wishes,

Antony

Royal Navy Story:

Thomas Cochrane served in the Royal Navy with distinction during the Napoleonic Wars. But later his reputation was destroyed after he was falsely jailed for fraud. He was stripped of his naval rank and because he was a serving politician lost his parliamentary seat.

Amazingly, not all was lost for Thomas. He joined the Chilean, Brazilian and Greeks navies to assist them in their fights for independence.

Later on, in 1832, he received a Royal pardon and restoration of his former naval rank.

Week 5 - Weird UK Laws

Goodday Roy,

Half way through basic training already! Wow. You're amazing, brilliant and you've totally got this.

I know I won't be there at your passing out ceremony due to limited tickets, but I want you to know that I will be thinking of you.

Your hard work, dedication and passion to the Royal Navy make them exceptionally lucky to have you.

In this week's email, I'm sharing with you some of the UK's weirdest laws.

1. It is illegal to give alcohol to a child under the age of 5 years old, unless it's prescribed by a doctor.

    What I want to know is why any doctor would want to get children drunk?

2. It is illegal to gamble, swear or behave in a disorderly manner in a library.

3. It is illegal to dress up as a Police Officer or to dress up as a member of the Armed Forces. You can actually be sent to prison for breaking this law.

4. It is illegal to be drunk and in charge of a child or cow. However the law doesn't protect plants or other animals - only children and cows.

5. Apparently it is illegal to fly a kite in public. If so, what's the purpose of having a kite?

6. Taxi drivers have a legal responsibility to ask passengers if they've had or got the plague or smallpox. I think the law probably needs updating now to include COVID-19.

7. Being homeless or begging is technically illegal. The law was past 1824, after we won a war with Napoleon and the French. Lawmakers of the time were worried about a post-war influx of idle and disorderly Persons, Rogues and Vagabonds.

8. It is illegal to linger at a grave after the funeral. The last reported case of the enforcement of this law came in 2015, when a man stayed by the grave of his wife for 20 minutes after the funeral. The man was fined £160, which if you ask me is just cruel.

9. In law King Charles, or any reigning monarch has the right to claim ownership of any whale beached anywhere in the UK. I have no idea what he wants with whales, but it sounds very Moby Dick to me.

10. It is illegal to import Polish potatoes. Potatoes from anywhere else in the world are fine to import. It is thought that this law was passed due to a plant disease that could affect other crops.

Until Next Week, My Best Wishes,

Antony

Royal Navy Fact:

The first Royal Navy ship to have armour, an iron hull and to be steam powered was the HMS Warrior in 1861. What a sight of power and might the ship must have been to see!

Week 6 - Would You Rather?
Hey Roy,

This week is all about: Would You Rather? Here's the WYRs and my responses. If you get time, email me back with yours. But as always, no pressure to email back, I can only imagine how gruelling the daily routine must be for you.

Would you rather be a badger with no fur or a horse that's missing a leg?
A horse with a missing leg. Horses are generally owned by people with money, so my owners could get me a prosthetic leg made.

Would you rather be a dinosaur that can talk or a pony that can dance?
This is a hard one. If I were a dinosaur that could talk, I could sell interviews and my story to the press. But if I were the pony that could dance, I could do a sell-out stadium tour.

The dinosaur. No the pony. I can't decide on this one.

Would you rather be blind or deaf?
Deaf. Although I'd miss music terribly, I think I'd struggle more with not being able to see the faces of people that I love.

Would you rather live for one day, but it be filled with joy or live for eternity but be miserable?
The live for one day for sure.

Would you rather be able to read minds (telepathy) or be able to move objects with your mind (telekinesis)?
Move objects with my mind, it would be more convenient and I am essentially lazy.

Would you rather win £100m on the EuroMillions or find true love?
True love, every time.

Would you rather be too hot or too cold?
Too hot. There are things I can do to cool myself down. Plus I really hate the cold.

Would you rather lose the ability to speak or lose the ability to read?
The ability to read. There are audio books these days and often books are made into films and radio shows. I would hate not to be able to express my thoughts, ideas, desires and dreams with others.

Would you rather be incredibly creative or incredibly rich?
Incredibly creative. Money isn't *that* important to me.

Would you rather be the smartest person in any room or the funniest person in any room?
Definitely the funniest. I love the sound of laughter and knowing that it came from something I said or did would make me extremely happy.

Would you rather be a donkey with one eye or a penguin that is allergic to fish?
A donkey with one eye. I'd get a sparkly eye patch, a wooden peg leg and become the first donkey pirate.

Would you rather have an annoying song stuck in your head forever (think Cheeky Girls) or always have an itch you can't reach?
Having an annoying song stuck on repeat in my head would drive me mad. So it would have to be the itch.

Would you rather lose an arm or a leg?
I'm quite attached to both my arms and legs. If I say arm, I'd lose my ability to do quite a lot of things for myself. But if I say leg, I'd lose my ability to walk, dance and mobilise independently. Then again, I could always get a wheelchair. So I'd have to say: Take my leg.

Would you rather lose your kindness or your ability to forgive?
This is a really tough one. I value my kindness greatly. But I imagine that if I couldn't forgive people I'd become quite cynical and bitter. So I would have to lose my kindness.

Would you rather have your own outer space theme park or a zoo that included mythical creatures?
Definitely the zoo. I'd love to see unicorns, lamacorns, dragons, merpeople, etc.

Write Soon,

Antony

Royal Navy Story:

The history of women in the Royal Navy is fascinating. In 1917, the *Women's Royal Naval Service* was established due to the outbreak of World War 1. After the war it was disbanded.

But the *Women's Royal Naval Service* was re-established in 1939 due the outbreak of World War 2.

The *Women's Royal Naval Service* continued to exist until 1993, when women were finally allowed to join the Royal Navy and serve on ships.

However it could be argued that women still have some way to go in achieving full equality with their male counterparts, as currently they aren't allowed to serve in the Royal Marines.

Week 7 - Most Common Myths
Hello Roy,

Week 7. I'm sure whatever challenges you have faced so far, the ones you currently face and the challenges to come you can meet. Keep going, you're nearly there now. The many rewards that will follow are as a direct result of you overcoming these challenges. I promise you that it will be worth it. I see you achieving great things.

This week my email is all about myths. A myth is a widely held belief or idea that is factually incorrect. They are usually told to us by our parents, other relatives and sometimes even by our friends.

#1: We only use 10% of our brain.
According to brain scans of people undertaking complex mental tasks up to 35% of their brains were in use.

#2: Go outside with wet hair in the Autumn or Winter and you'll catch a cold.
I couldn't ascertain where this myth came from. But it probably started off from some well meaning mum to her children. Going outside with wet hair when it's cold is unpleasant. But there is no evidence that doing so makes you more susceptible to the cold virus or that doing so weakens your immune system in any way.

#3: Bulls get angry at the sight of a red cape.
For a start bulls are colour blind. Apparently it's the movement of the cape that makes them angry and charge. Even then this is learned behaviour, learned from the humans who look after them.

#4: Goldfish only have a 3 second memory.
This is just plain incorrect and has been discredited in countless scientific studies.

#5: Dogs can only see in black and white.
While it is true that dogs can't see the full range of colours that a human can, they can certainly see more than just black and white.

#6: That the French General Napoleon was short.
Napoleon was approximately 5 foot and 5 inches, which for a man at the time was considered to be average height.

#7: That you should wait 24 hours before reporting someone missing to the Police.
The truth is quite the opposite. The first 48 hours someone goes missing is crucial for finding them. So if someone in your life ever goes missing, report it to the Police straight away.

#8: If you are cold, drinking alcohol raises your core body temperature.
The opposite is true.

#9: Bats are blind.
Another false fact. Their eyesight is actually rumoured to be better than human's eyesight.

#10: Chameleons change the colour of their skin to blend in with their environment as an act of camouflage.
Untrue. They do it to help regulate body temperature or to communicate with others of their species.

#11: It's okay to eat food that's been on the floor for less than 5 seconds (the 5 second rule).
This is a lie that I think we tell ourselves to make ourselves feel better. The truth is that as soon as food touches the floor, anything that is on the floor instantly contaminates the food.

#12: You should pee on someone if they have been stung by a jellyfish.
Wrong. It probably wouldn't be appreciated either. Instead, put the affected body part under a hot tap.

#13: When flipping a coin the odds are 50/50.
Testing this theory, researchers discovered that the odds were ever so slightly higher that the coin will land on the face it had started on.

#14: Everything that is alive will die.
Actually there are immortal jellyfish.

#15: That mice like cheese.
Although they probably would give cheese a nibble, they prefer foods that are higher in carbohydrates like grains, fruits and seeds.

That's it for another week. Massive Hugs and Write Soon,

Antony

Royal Navy Story:

World War 1 saw arguably the biggest Naval battle in recent history. The battle was between the Royal Navy (UK) and the Germans. It is now known as the Battle of Jutland.

The Battle of Jutland took place between 31st May to 1st June 1916 in the North Sea, near Denmark.

The Royal Navy had the bigger fleet with 151 combat ships. The make up consisted of 28 dreadnought battleships, 9 battlecruisers, 8 armoured cruisers, 26 light cruisers, 78 destroyers, 1 minelayer and 1 seaplane carrier.

The German fleet consisted of 99 combat ships. The make up consisted of 16 dreadnought battleships, 5 battlecruisers, 6 pre-dreadnought battleships, 11 light cruisers and 61 torpedo-boats.

The German's sought to divide the British fleet in order to gain the tactical advantage. The tack tick ultimately failed. However there were three engagements with a massive loss of life and ships on both sides.

But the Royal Navy's strategy was a longterm one. They needed to block the German fleet, to prevent access to Britain and the Atlantic ocean. Ultimately the Royal Navy's strategy was successful.

Week 8 - Gay Animals
Ahoy Sailor Roy,

Have I mentioned recently that I'm proud to call you my dear friend? Well just in case I haven't: I'm proud to call you my dear friend. You are one of only a few friends that I would trust with my life and one of only a few friends that has a front door key to my apartment.

Homosexuality has been found in more than 1,500 species of animals through behavioural observation research studies. Here's ten animals were gay liaisons or relationships exist:

1. **Lions**
   Male lions in Africa have been observed disregarding available lionesses in order to form their own same-sex prides.

   These same males have also been seen mounting one another and doing other actions commonly associated with male to female mating interactions.

2. **Cheetahs**
   When cheetahs bond together, they do for life. Cheetah partners spend about 93% of their time together and male same-sex partners are quite common.

   The two bonded males will groom one another (usually a sign of partnered straight cheetahs), defend each other in fights and get anxiety if separated. Once reunited the male cheetahs will face-rub one another, mount one another (fully erect) and stutter (a sexual excitement vocalisation).

   It is estimated that 27-40% of wild male cheetahs live with same-sex partners and that 16-19% of wild male cheetahs live in a same-sex trio.

3. **Elephants**
Male elephants have been known to touch other males with their trunks (elephants see touch as essential for creating and maintaining a deep bond), kissing other males (inserting their trunk into the other elephant's mouth) and even male on male sex (mounting).

Relationships between two male elephants (usually one older and one younger) have been known to last for years.

4. **Emus**
Emus travel together in pairs. Male emus have been seen making the same mating behaviours as females do to males. This includes: circling a passive male, patches of bare skin turning light blue (on both males), the passive male stretching his neck, erecting his feathers and swaying from side to side and the dominant male rubbing his breast against the other male's rump.

5. **Flamingos**
Flamingos are sociable animals, living together in large colonies. During mating season, they split off into smaller groups and perform synchronised displays. They choose their mate and stay together for the season. They generally have a new mate for every mating season.

The most famous same-sex flamingo couple is Carlos and Fernando. In 2007, when they had been together for five years, they adopted an abandoned chick. They fed it and raised it as their own. Homosexuality is said to be very common with flamingos.

6. **Penguins**
Same-sex penguins have been seen performing mating calls to one another and intertwining their necks. There have been a few gay penguin couples in zoos around the world that have been given abandoned eggs to raise as their own chicks. They have raised these chicks successfully.

Famous penguin couples include: Roy & Silo, Inca & Rayas and Buddy & Pedro. Each of these couples is a separate subspecies of penguin, meaning that several subspecies of penguin have documented gay penguins.

7. **Dolphins**
Several subspecies of dolphin have gay or bisexual dolphins. One researcher discovered the incredible seventeen year gay relationship between two male dolphins.

Researchers have also found pods of all male dolphins who share sexual and romantic experiences together. Dolphins are known to be highly flirtatious and sexualised.

Male dolphins have been known to engage in masturbation of other males. Same-sex dolphins engage in long foreplay, with the sexual act only lasting a short time. Male dolphins regardless of their sexuality tend to be aggressive and violent towards their partners during sex.

8. **Foxes**
Foxes are nocturnal animals, which out of breeding season live alone. They often share territory where there is a dominant male. The dominant male will mount a same-sex subordinate doggy style.

During breeding season foxes generally live in a den, either as a mated straight couple or a male with several young females. I guess you could say foxes are more bisexual than gay.

9. **Bats**
Bats are said to have the highest percentage of gayness, above all other animals, including humans. Both male and female bats can be gay with their behaviours including: affection, sexual activity and bonding.

There are several subspecies of bats that are gay including Vampire Bats, Fruit Bats and Flying Fox Bats.

10. Cats

Tom cats (males) have been known to engage in same-sex interludes. As well as humping one another, they have been seen spooning when they sleep and grooming one another.

However cats are not picky, they will get together with anyone. Even members of their family, such as their mothers, fathers, sisters, brothers, sons and daughters.

I'm sure Russell (one of my cats) is gay. He loves any sort of affection, and despite being the bigger of the two cats, he's not at all dominant.

Best Wishes,

Antony

Royal Navy Fact:

In 'Operation Neptune,' also known as 'The Normandy Landings,' which took place on 6th June 1944, during World War 2, the Royal Navy delivered 130,000 men safely onto the beaches of Normandy.

Week 9 - A List of Qualities in People that Inspire Me
Hello My Friend,

Just one week to go now, then you pass out of basic training for the Royal Navy. I bet it has been an incredible and life changing journey.

This week it's a short one. Here is a list of qualities in people that inspire me:

Accepting	**Authentic**	Balanced in their thinking
Battle their inner demons	**Believe in fairness and equality**	**Brings joy to others**
Can have a presence on entering a room or blend into the background in social situations	Captivating Storyteller	**Careful in their actions**
Cares about others	**Comfortable with themselves**	Confident yet humble
Connects emotionally with others	Creative	**Describes their own thoughts & feelings through words well**
Determined	Diplomatic	**Empathetic**
Enthusiastic	Flawed	**Funny**
Generous	**Good communicator**	**Has others following them**
Honest	**Independent**	**Intelligent**
Is a Collaborator	**Is a Doer**	Is a Dreamer

Is Kind	**Knows when, who and why to ask for help**	**Makes others feel comfortable**
Motivational	**Non-judgemental**	**Occasionally vulnerable**
One-step ahead of others	Optimistic	**Passionate**
Patient	Relaxed in new situations	**Self-aware**
Shares their knowledge and wisdom	Sincere	**Stands up for the rights of others**
Supports & helps others	Unconventional	Values community
Wants others to reach their potential	Willing to fight for a cause	**Works hard**

As I have told you many times: you inspire me. The qualities above in **bold** apply to you.

Just one more week to go now. I would imagine that if you haven't already got details of your first deployment by now, you'll be getting these soon.

Be Safe. Love & Hugs,

Antony

Week 10 - Future Technology to Be Excited About
Hi Roy!

Many, many congratulations on completing your final week of basic training and for successfully passing out.

I'm so stoked for you. Words cannot express how happy I am to see a dear friend reach their goal and achieve something they've dreamed about since childhood. As I write this email, I'm literally bursting with pride for you.

This email is about the future and specifically future technology that will transform the way we live our lives.

First off we have robots. They're better than staff (because you don't have to pay them or give them time off). Imagine never having to do housework again. My idea of bliss.

Next we have space travel and exploration. Imagine space holidays, how awesome would that be? Currently you have to be incredibly wealthy to visit space (think Richard Branson). But imagine if you could go on holiday to a hotel on the Moon for the same price as a flight to Spain.

The self-driving car, boat, plane or spaceship. This would be a fantastic way to travel and I would mean I could nap on the drive home from work.

The internet becomes truly global. Everyone in the world has access wherever they are and for free. Regardless of affordability. This would go a long way towards true equality in humanity.

There is enough food for everyone and it could even be free or at least very cheap. Technology could bring better food growing and production methods.

Virtual Reality headsets are currently in development that would trick your brain into believing you are where the headset shows you. More than just a screen showing you a place, you'd be able to see everything, hear the appropriate sounds, smell the smells of the place, taste the food and even reach out and touch this virtual reality environment.

Artificial intelligence will enable us to work less. At least I hope. This is more than just being able to automate basic tasks. Computers will develop to the point where they can solve humanity's greatest and most complex problems.

You're talking about smart drugs that can target the root cause of a disease, better solutions to climate change, more secure cyber security, computers that can compose music, poetry, stories and films.

In fact, thinking about it, illness and disease could be a thing of the past with artificial intelligence. Hospitals could be shut down, doctors and nurses made a thing of the past.

There's even the potential for artificial intelligence to work out how to bring back extinct species of plants and animals - like the dinosaurs.

Starships could be developed that people live and explore the galaxy in.

In the future we will be able to grow new cells, tissues, organs, bones and other body parts as required. With no chance of our bodies rejecting them. This could potentially lead to some or all humans becoming immortal.

Time travel. Okay, you're probably rolling your eyes right now reading this. But if we can learn to travel through space, who's to say we won't discover the ability to travel through time? Imagine being able to meet and converse with anyone throughout all of history. That would be awesome.

The future brings some exciting opportunities, but it is also likely to bring some challenging and complex problems for humanity.

I don't think I've ever told you this: But I write these emails in advance. By now, we'll have spoken and you'll have told me all about your first deployment.

I'm going to continue these weekly emails, whenever you're away. To hopefully delight, entertain, make you laugh and occasionally even inspire you.

My Best Wishes,

Antony

Royal Navy Fact:

In 1963, the Royal Navy commissioned its first nuclear powered submarine, the HMS Dreadnought.

Week 11 - 25 Date Ideas

Hi Roy,

Welcome to week 1 of your first deployment. I hope this email finds you well and that you are settling in onboard the ship.

As Oscar Wilde once said:

"Keep love in your heart. A life without it is like a sunless garden when the flowers are dead. The consciousness of loving and being loved brings a warmth and a richness to life that nothing else can bring."

Now, I know love will be the last thing on your mind right now. But it is an important area of our lives and one that we shouldn't neglect.

So here's 25 date ideas:

1. Go to the cinema
2. Go for a walk
3. Take a picnic to the local park
4. Go ice skating
5. Take a dance class together
6. Play strip poker
7. Visit a zoo
8. Visit an art gallery
9. Visit a theme park
10. Go bowling
11. Visit another town or city
12. Visit a castle, stately home or other old place
13. Go book shopping together
14. Visit a beach
15. Try out a new restaurant
16. Have a board games night
17. Go paintballing
18. Visit an escape room

19. Have a cosy night in - get snacks and watch a film together

20. Go kayaking

21. Volunteer for a worthy cause

22. Visit a museum or art gallery

23. Go rock climbing

24. Go axe throwing

25. Take a mystery tour in the car

Best Wishes,

Antony

Royal Navy Fact:

Future Royal Navy Staff are trained at HMS Raleigh in Torpoint, near Plymouth, UK. Basic training is an intensive 10 week programme including: discipline, physical exercise, firearms training and lectures. After this staff begin professional training in a field they have agreed with their superiors.

Week 12 - How to Fight a Shark
Hey Roy,

Picture the scene, you're on a ship but forced to jump into the cold ocean waters as it's sinking. It isn't long before you attract some unwanted attention. Sharks. They begin circling you and you know it won't be long before you have to fight for your life.

Here's my survival guide to this scenario:

1. Identify the type of sharks circling you. I'm sad to say that most sharks are carnivorous and would seek to gobble you up. However bonnethead sharks are vegetarian for 62% of the time, eating seagrass.

2. Don't play dead. Sharks are smart and will know you are faking it. They're also not opposed to eating dead humans.

3. Remain calm, keep eyes on them at all times and make sudden sporadic movements in an attempt to scare the sharks.

4. Look around for any weapons or things that could be used as weapons. Use whatever you find in your battle with the sharks.

5. If it's hand to fin battle, focus your attention on the vulnerable parts of the sharks: their eyes, noses and gills. Avoid the mouth at all costs due to the sharp teeth.

6. I once heard a story of a man who was attacked by a shark and successfully fended it off by punching it in the nose. I don't know how true this story is. But desperate times call for desperate measures, so definitely worth a try.

7. If you see a dolphin or a pod of dolphins call on them for help. They generally like humans and sharks are apparently afraid of them.

8. Don't under any circumstances try to swim away. Sharks will see this as a sign of weakness and besides which, they can swim quicker than you. So trying to swim away would be a pointless waste of energy.

9. If all else fails, try to reason with the sharks. Explain to them the reasons they shouldn't eat you. You could even tell them jokes or sing them a song in exchange for sparing your life.

That's it for this week.

Big Hugs,

Antony

Royal Navy Fact:

The Royal Navy is responsible for the Continuous At Sea Deterrent (CASD). The CASD is also known as the nuclear deterrent. This is a series of submarines equipped with nuclear Trident II missiles.

Week 13 - How to Woo a Turtle

Hello My Friend,

We never know what's going to happen in life. One day, you might need to woo a turtle. I know you wouldn't know where to start. But don't worry, I've got your back. Here's how to woo a turtle.

First you've got to flirt with the turtle. Make eye contact, give it your cutest smile and tell it your funniest joke. Turtles love a good laugh.

Next, invite it out to dinner. Most turtles are omnivores meaning they eat both meat and vegetables. But I would personally avoid any restaurants that serve turtle as a main course or side dish. Remember to dress to impress on this date.

On the date pay the turtle complements, listen to what they say and try to find common interests to talk about. Ensure you're always honest with the turtle, as they are good judges of character and can spot a liar.

At the end of the date thank the turtle for a good time and ask for its number.

Ha ha, so this was just a bit of fun to write and for you to read.

But these same tips above could be applied to a man or woman, or any species of animal really. I'm not sure if they'd work on aliens, as I've never met one to give it a try.

My Best Wishes,

Antony

Royal Navy Fact: It has around 32,360 active personnel.

Week 14 - Some of the Most Amazing Jobs in the World
Hey Roy,

I hope this email finds you well. This week I'm going to tell you about some of the most amazing jobs in the world.

Serving in the Armed Forces - You already know why serving in the armed forces is such a brilliant job. It gives you the opportunity to learn new skills, to travel and to make a difference to other people's lives.

Doctor, Nurse or Other Health Professional - These people physically, mentally and emotionally heal others. They often save lives. How incredible is that?

Zoologist - These people study animals and their behaviours. They are often responsible for setting up programmes to protect endangered species.

Astronaut - These lucky people get to see our lovely planet from space. What a wonderful day at work!

Writer or Author - These people have a magical ability to take us to places we've never even dared to imagine, introduce us to some fantastic characters and make us feel deep emotions. Just from some symbols scribbled on pages in a book.

Scientist or Researcher - While these might not seem that exciting and you might be thinking: *What are you talking about?* Hear me out. Imagine being the Scientist or Researcher who discovers a cure for cancer. That would be a pretty awesome day at work.

Until Next Week,

Antony

Week 15 - The Cycle of Change
Hi Roy,

Another week. Another email.

Change is defined as a process through which something or someone becomes different. Change is a part of life. It brings with it challenges, but also opportunities.

A theory of change is called The Cycle of Change. It was developed in the 1980s by Prochaska and DiClemente. They studied how smokers made changes to their behaviour. They came up with this process:

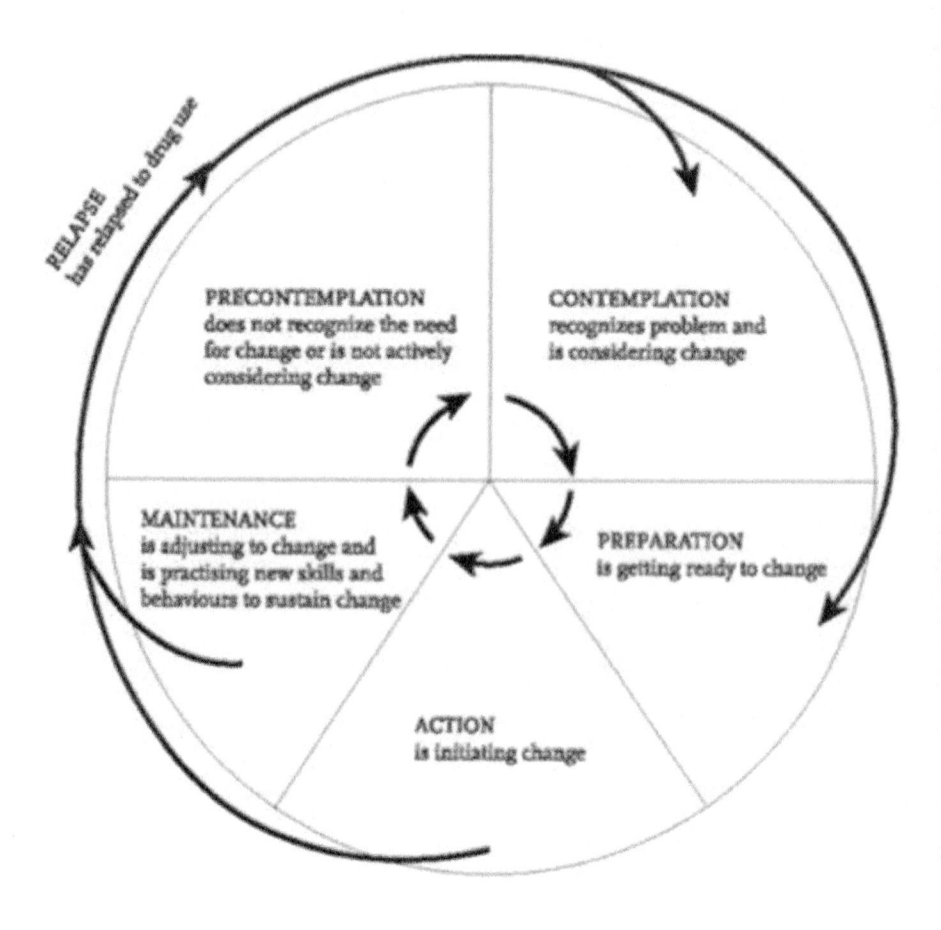

RELAPSE has relapsed to drug use

PRECONTEMPLATION does not recognize the need for change or is not actively considering change

CONTEMPLATION recognizes problem and is considering change

PREPARATION is getting ready to change

ACTION is initiating change

MAINTENANCE is adjusting to change and is practising new skills and behaviours to sustain change

1. Precontemplation is the first stage in The Cycle of Change. In the precontemplation stage a person is happy with their current behaviour.

2. Contemplation is the second stage and is when someone is thinking about the pros and cons of their current behaviour. They will be realising the impact their behaviour is having on themselves and others.

3. The Preparation stage is next and is where someone starts to plan for the change. This usually starts with them setting a goal or goals.

4. The Action stage is next and in this stage the person puts their plan into action.

5. Maintenance is all about maintaining the change. According to Prochaska and DiClemente the maintenance stage should take around 4-6 months to complete.

6. Lapse is a stage often added into this model. It describes a one-off event where someone goes back to their old pattern of behaviour.

7. The Relapse stage involves the person going completely back to the old behaviour. Back to where they started.

You went through this process and change really started to happen for you once you set your goal: To enlist in the Royal Navy.

You gave up smoking, started attending the gym to improve your fitness and lose weight and learned more about the Royal Navy.

You implemented several changes at once, when most people struggle making one change which is really impressive.

Write Soon,

Antony

Week 16 - Things To Look Forward To
Hi Roy,

This week is all-about things to look forward to. We all need things to look forward to. For you, it's likely to be learning new things on the ship. But it's okay to welcome time off and plan things to look forward to.

Here's some ideas of things you could plan to do when you're next home:

1. Go for dinner with family and friends. Even better, try out a new restaurant.

2. Visit a zoo, museum or art gallery.

3. Go travelling.

4. Go out dancing.

5. Go to a music gig or theatre show.

6. Go see a comedian or go to a comedy night.

7. Make special memories with your significant other.

8. Get tickets to sit in the audience of your favourite TV show.

9. Go skydiving.

10. Do something for a veterans charity.

11. Play games with your online friends.

12. Treat yourself to some luxurious self-care, book yourself a massage, aromatherapy or reiki session.

Best Wishes,

Antony

Week 17 - Facts About Castles
Hey Roy,

How are you doing?

Castles are ancient structures once used to protect Kings, Lords and other important people. There are some beautiful castles here in the UK. Here's some fascinating facts about castles:

1. Windsor Castle is said to be the biggest castle in the UK. At over 900 years old, it is still in active use today. Not for defensive purposes as originally intended, but where some of the Royal family hang out.

2. Stone castles took on average 10 years to build. Before castles were made out of stone, they were made out of wood.

3. Castles usually had no toilets. Just a wooden bench with a hole further down the wall to the outside.

4. You can rent a castle out, usually for weddings or other occasions. But they carry a hefty price tag.

5. Castles were often impenetrable. So the only way to capture one was by siege. Stopping food and water from entering the castle and then waiting until those in the castle had run out of resources. People in the castles would be forced to eat rats to survive.

6. A famous castle - The Tower of London had a dual use. It was a palace for Elizabth I when she was young to keep her safe. Later it was used as a prison, housing Guy Fawkes after his failed attempt to blow up the Houses of Parliament.

7. Some castles have a murder hole. This is a hole in the ceiling of the castle near the entrance, through which would be poured boiling oil or water on enemy attackers.

8. Castles with water wells were vulnerable to enemies poisoning the water supply.

My Royal Navy Friend

9. There are currently 427 castles or ruins of castles in Wales. However, historic documentation indicates that in the past there were more than 600.

10. Chepstow Castle is nearly 1,000 years old and is thought to be one of the first stone castles in Wales.

11. King Henry VIII built a number of castles during his reign due to the threat of invasion by France. These castles stretched along the coast from Cornwall to Kent.

12. Historically, castles weren't just a trend in the UK. It is estimated that there were around 100,000 castles across Europe at one time. Many were either destroyed or fell into disrepair.

13. The invention of gunpowder made castles a lot less secure. To combat this invention, defenders would send soldiers and knights out to battle the enemy on open fields, rather than hiding behind the now vulnerable castle walls. Staying inside the castle after the invention of gunpowder was considered a last resort.

14. Edinburgh Castle has been under siege more times than any other castle in Europe. According to historic records there have been 23 sieges.

15. There are a lot of ghost stories associated with castles.

Write Soon,

Antony

Royal Navy Fact: The HMS Victory is famous for the Battle of Trafalgar in 1805. The Battle was between the Royal Navy (UK) and the combined naval fleets of the French and Spanish. Lord Nelson led the Royal Navy fleet and was outnumbered, but Nelson's strategy ultimately proved effective at beating the larger combined fleet.

Week 18 - Dad Jokes
Ahoy Sailor,

I hope all is well with you. This week's email is all about dad jokes. You know the ones - they are so terrible but you can't help but laugh. May these at least bring a smile to your face. Let's get started:

What do you call a fish wearing a bowtie?
Sofishticated

How do you follow Will Smith in the snow?
You follow the fresh prints.

What did the ocean say to the beach?
Nothing, it just waved.

I don't trust those trees. They seem kind of shady.

Why don't eggs tell jokes? They'd crack each other up.

This graveyard looks overcrowded. People must be dying to get in.

Why didn't the skeleton climb the mountain? It didn't have the guts.

You think swimming with sharks is expensive? Swimming with sharks cost me an arm and a leg.

A cheeseburger walks into a bar. The bartender says, "Sorry, we don't serve food here."

I'm on a seafood diet. I see food and I eat it.

Why did the scarecrow win an award?
Because he was outstanding in his field.

I've got a great joke about construction, but I'm still working on it.

I'm so good at sleeping, I can do it with my eyes closed!

What did the vet say to the cat?
How are you feline?

What happens when a strawberry gets run over crossing the street?
Traffic jam.

What do you call a pony with a sore throat?
A little hoarse.

What's a robot's favourite snack?
Computer chips.

Wanna hear a joke about paper?
Never mind—it's tearable.

I could tell a joke about pizza, but it's a little cheesy.

What's an astronaut's favourite part of a computer?
The space bar.

Today at the bank, an old lady asked me to check her balance.
So I pushed her over.

How many stormtroopers does it take to change a lightbulb?
None. Because they are all on the dark side.

Why did the man fall in the well?
Because he couldn't see that well.

What does a vegetarian zombie eat?
G-R-A-I-N-S.

I'm afraid of the stairs, they're always up to something.

What do you call an elephant in a telephone box?
Stuck.

What did one traffic light say to the other?
Stop looking, I'm changing.

Why don't skeletons go trick or treating?
Because they have no body to go with.

Best Wishes,

Antony

Royal Navy Story:

Sir Francis Drake is perhaps the most famous English Sailor, Explorer and Fleet Commander in British history. His story is taught in primary schools in the UK.

It was Elizabethan times and Queen Elizabeth I was on the English throne. Queen Elizabeth I instructed Drake to circumnavigate the globe. There was a lot of political tension at the time between the English and the Spanish.

Queen Elizabeth I told Drake that he could attack, loot and sink as many Spanish ships as he liked along the way. But to make sure not to leave survivors who could identify his ship as English. Drake was successful in his endeavour.

By this time, King Philip II of Spain had planned to invade England to expand his empire and to dethrone Queen Elizabeth I. In 1587, Drake led a British fleet and raided Spain's harbour at Cádiz, destroying a lot of the Spanish fleet. It took the Spanish about a year to rebuild their fleet.

In 1588, a Spanish armada of ships set sail for English shores. Queen Elizabeth I, called Drake to assemble a fleet and meet the Spanish fleet. The English fleet engaged with the Spanish fleet in the English Channel and successfully thought them off.

Week 19 - Do Aliens Exist?
Hey Roy,

Aliens. Little green men. Martians. Extraterrestrials. Those dudes from outer space. They have many names, but do aliens actually exist?

The odds are that aliens do actually exist. Our galaxy alone has around 400 billion stars like the sun. Add to this the vast, infinite rest of the universe and it's unlikely that Earth is the only planet that supports life.

So, what would life look like? Life can take many forms, from single celled organisms to more complex life like plants, animals and humans. Recent research has found that life might even exist in our solar system on Mars or Jupiter.

Life on Mars and Jupiter is expected to be single celled or small multiple celled organisms due to the environmental conditions on the planets.

But what about more complex life? Like aliens in sci-fi TV shows and films? They could easily exist and be flying around in space, in their spaceships with their futuristic technology.

Why haven't we been able to make contact or meet them yet? There could be several reasons for this including:
- Aliens have chosen not to visit us. This could possibly be due to the lack of spaceship parking availability and parking prices.
- Aliens haven't yet got the technology to travel through space.
- Aliens have seen our films about them and worry about how they would be treated.
- Aliens have been banned from visiting or communicating with Earth by some intergalactic council.
- Aliens can't breathe oxygen, or are allergic to water or have some other health reason for not visiting.
- Aliens don't visit as they don't speak English or any other of the Earth's languages.
- We are in some isolated part of the galaxy.

- Aliens could have already visited us, but in disguise as plumbers.
- Aliens could be hibernating.
- Aliens may have visited Earth at a time in our distant past (think age of the dinosaurs) and realised that there weren't any theme parks or tourist attractions.
- Perhaps we are sending out messages into the universe on the wrong channel.

That's all for this week. Big Hugs,

Antony

Royal Navy Fact:

The Royal Navy isn't just a defensive force to keep the UK safe. It is also involved in diplomatic and NATO (North Atlantic Treaty Organization) activities. It is also often involved in humanitarian aid operations across the world.

My Royal Navy Friend

Week 20 - Solve These Puzzles
Hi Roy,

This week it's puzzle time! Get your brain into gear and solve these puzzles:

Word Search
Find these words in the grid below: **Sailor, Navy, Duck, Shark, Dinosaur, Alien, Pineapple.**

E	L	P	P	A	E	N	I	P	A
N	A	Y	M	N	O	R	S	H	A
A	S	D	S	N	I	D	F	P	L
E	I	S	H	O	U	I	X	D	U
P	R	S	A	T	Y	N	C	I	N
A	D	P	R	I	X	K	C	U	D
L	I	A	N	A	L	I	N	E	A
I	N	S	N	V	S	O	Z	O	P
E	O	W	A	P	P	A	R	A	P
N	Q	I	V	I	W	R	I	L	W
O	L	I	Y	A	L	S	E	L	O
D	N	I	X	O	L	O	N	I	O
I	A	C	P	L	I	I	R	A	U
C	U	R	U	A	S	O	N	I	D
D	S	H	A	R	A	P	P	L	C
K	S	D	C	E	S	H	A	R	K

Riddles
Solve these riddles:

1. What has to be broken before you can use it?

2. I'm tall when I'm young, and I'm short when I'm old. What am I?

3. What is full of holes but still holds water?

4. What is always in front of you but can't be seen?

5. What can you break, even if you never pick it up or touch it?

6. What goes up but never comes down?

Which Answer is Correct?
1. How long did the oldest known elephant live for?
   A) 86 Years   B) 147 Years   C) 142 Years   D) 150 Years

2. How many rings are on the Olympic flag?
   A) 1   B) 7   C) 5   D) 0

3. In darts, what's the most points you can score with a single throw?
   A) 100   B) 60   C) 80   D) 90

4. How many holes are on a standard bowling ball?
   A) 5   B) 3   C) 6   D) 9

5. Are giant pandas a type of bear?
   A) Yes   B) No

6. What are the main colours on the flag of Spain?
   A) Yellow & Green   B) Red & Yellow

Answers to these puzzles are on the next page.

The Answers

E	L	P	P	A	E	N	I	P	A
N	A	Y	M	N	O	R	S	H	A
A	S	D	S	N	I	D	F	P	L
E	I	S	H	O	U	I	X	D	U
P	R	S	A	T	Y	N	C	I	N
A	D	P	R	I	X	K	C	U	D
L	I	A	N	A	L	I	N	E	A
I	N	S	N	V	S	O	Z	O	P
E	O	W	A	P	P	A	R	A	P
N	Q	I	V	I	W	R	I	L	W
O	L	I	Y	A	L	S	E	L	O
D	N	I	X	O	L	O	N	I	O
I	A	C	P	L	I	I	R	A	U
C	U	R	U	A	S	O	N	I	D
D	S	H	A	R	A	P	P	L	C
K	S	D	C	E	S	H	A	R	K

1. An egg
2. A candle
3. A sponge
4. The Future
5. A promise
6. Your age

Correct Answers: 1. A, 2. C, 3. B, 4. B, 5. A, 6. B.

Page 54

Week 21 - The Best-Selling Objects of All Time
Hey Roy,

How's it going? I hope you enjoyed the puzzles last week. This week let's look at the best-selling objects of all time:

1. Food and Drink - It is essential to our survival. I reckon that food is probably among the best selling objects of all time. I couldn't find figures to back up my claim online. But since humans have existed we've needed to eat and drink. The amount of food and drink consumed is incalculable. It was happening before records even began. So yeah, number 1 has got to be food and drink.

2. Oil and Gas - For the past 50 years, these natural resources have been making their owners a staggering £2.3 billions of pure profit every day. They are currently considered essential for energy and fuel. But times are changing. Oil and gas are slowly being used up. Many economies are looking at renewables, which are cleaner and greener ways of producing energy.

3. Medicines - There's a reason why the pharmaceutical industry is worth billions, if not trillions of pounds. Literally billions of medicines are consumed across the globe each year. Making medicines one the best-selling objects of all time. Probably not surprising but in 2021 and 2022, the best-selling medicines were COVID-19 vaccinations.

4. Illegal Drugs - This unregulated and untaxed market is worth billions, if not trillions of pounds every year. Because of the illegal nature of these substances there are lots of unknowns. We're not sure how many people are involved with the making/growing, distribution, selling or using of these substances. But despite the harms to individuals, families and communities there is data to suggest that illegal drugs are popular and could be considered one of the best-selling objects around.

5. Alcohol - A lot of people like a drink and data suggests that this is a growing market. This is despite the harms to an individual's physical, mental and emotional health. Making alcohol a best-selling object around the world.

6. Tobacco / Cigarettes - This industry has a growing market, despite the risks to health that have been widely reported and numerous public health campaigns about the dangers of smoking. There isn't yet good reliable data about the numbers of people globally that have switched from smoking to vaping, but I'd hazard a guess that vaping is not far behind smoking in terms of being a growing market.

7. Disney Products - Disney is estimated to be worth well over $150 billion. Making their films, merchandise, theme parks and hotels some of the most popular and best-selling objects of all time.

8. Cars - There are around 67 millions cars sold worldwide each year. I couldn't get a figure for all time. In some parts of the world, these are not just for the wealthy, but for all and essential to survival.

9. The Bible - Over a billion copies of the bible have been printed and sold across the globe. It is the best-selling book of all time, much to the frustration of J.K Rowling.

10. The Star Wars Franchise - Sold to Disney for $4 billion. But it was a wise move for Disney, because once you take into account film sales and merchandise sales it will more than make its money back.

11. Apple Products - Apple has sold over 400 million iPads alone. Add to that its iPhones, Mac Books, Macs, accessories, other devices, Apps/Music and it is no surprise that it makes this list and is truly a global brand.

12. The Sony Playstation - More than 440 million devices sold.

Wow, most of the objects on that list were unexpected. Before I started this email I was thinking about things, like the bible. It was only when I started researching online that I discovered the resources (e.g. food, fuel, drugs and alcohol).

Best Wishes,

Antony

Royal Navy Fact:

In 1901 the Submarine Service was launched by the Royal Navy. Within the Royal Navy, it is often referred to as the *Silent Service*.

Week 22 - Some of the Most Impressive Inventions by Mankind

Hello My Friend,

Inventions change the world and the way we live our lives. Here are some of the most impressive inventions by mankind:

Language - Common understanding is what binds us together as human beings and makes us social animals. What's amazing is the variety of languages that developed across the world and that languages continue to evolve to this day.

Writing - Before writing information could only be passed on verbally and no doubt information was lost, or like chinese whispers, changed from one generation to the next.

Writing is an incredible invention if you think about it. One person can draw some scribbles on a page and someone else can interpret those scribbles to gain a perfect understanding of the writer's message. These two people, the writer and reader could be hundreds of years apart.

The Wheel - Wheels allowed the invention of carts and other vehicles to transport people and goods.

Irrigation - Enabled crops to be grown on a larger scale to allow bigger populations of people.

Hunting Weapons - These allowed early people to hunt wild animals for food and to use their fur coats for clothes.

Cement - This building material revolutionised buildings and also led to the development of other things such as pottery.

The Compass - This rather clever invention enabled people to find their way in the world and find their way home when they were lost. It enabled people to travel further than their local village and helped them develop maps.

The Aeroplane - Throughout time men and women have daydreamed about how magical it must be to fly in the sky like a bird. The aeroplane is the closest we have come to imitating this experience.

Images - I mean much more than just photos. I mean: drawings, diagrams, maps, paintings, process charts, data analyst charts, etc.

Videos - Another great way to inform, educate and even inspire. There's a reason why TikTok has exploded in popularity.

The Internet - The internet was invented by Sir Tim Berners-Lee, a British Computer Scientist. The internet is so impressive because of the amount of good it can do.

The Internet can connect people who are literally on the other side of the world, be a source of economic growth, inform, educate, entertain (think: Netflix, music & games), highlight important causes, allow an easy way for citizens to engage in local and national politics and even be good for the environment (think: eBooks and therefore less trees cut down to make paper).

Best Wishes,

Antony

Royal Navy Fact:

'Scurvy' is a disease caused by a lack of Vitamin C and was common on Royal Navy ships until 1790. Pioneer Gilbert Blane, who was Chairman of the Navy's Sick and Hurt Board, ordered fresh lemon juice to be given to all sailors on ships. It was so successful that it completely eliminated scurvy in the Royal Navy. Other navies across the world soon copied this to address their scurvy problem.

Week 23 - Facts About Disney that You Probably Didn't Know
Hi Roy,

How are you this week?

The Disney brand is global and worth more than £100 billion. It includes films, merchandise, theme parks and even Star Wars. Many people associate Disney with their childhood. Here are some facts about Disney that you probably didn't know:

The Films
Mothers in Disney films are underrepresented and this is said to be because Walt Disney's mother died prematurely.

To sell the idea of Snow White to his staff, Walt did a one man show, playing out the plot and all of the characters.

Snow White was a make-or-break film for Disney. If it had failed to captivate an audience (which it has done so for multiple generations), it would have bankrupted Walt and ended Disney. Luckily, the risk paid off. Just think of the many great films that Disney has made since Snow White. Imagine if these had never been made - a scary thought indeed.

One of the secrets to Disney's success has been buying up film companies and more recently rights and franchises.

Joss Whedon (think the Writer of the TV show *Buffy The Vampire Slayer*) was part of a team of writers brought in to make the Toy Story script better. He also came up with the character of the toy T-Rex dinosaur Rex.

In The Lion King, Simba was named Simba is the Swahili word for lion. This is not the only Disney film to name some of their characters in this way. In The Jungle Book, Baloo was named because Bhalu is the Hindi word for bear.

Walt Disney

Walt Disney never went to college or university but has three Masters level qualifications. They were awarded for his accomplishments. He had a Masters in Science from the University of Southern California, a Master of Arts from Yale University and a Masters of Arts from the prestigious Harvard University.

Walt Disney died prematurely at the age of 65 years old due to lung cancer. He was a smoker. There were persistent rumours that his body was cryogenically frozen so that he could be brought back to life in the future. However it is reported that his body was cremated.

The Theme Parks

In the 1950s, Walt Disney wanted to be on site where Disneyland was being built. So he built an apartment in the upstairs of the Fire Station on Main Street. In one of the windows, Walt placed a lamp and turned it on if he was in residence, so that people knew he was home. After he died the lamp remains always lit in remembrance of Walt.

The actors/actresses who play Disney characters in theme parks, have a number of rules they must obey. The rules include: never saying the word No, not being allowed to sit down, never break character and never point with their finger when giving directions.

Every year, some families ask to scatter the ashes of their beloved deceased relatives in the Disneyland theme parks. Disney always says no, but this hasn't stopped at least family from trying incognito.

In the theme parks and presumably the development studios Disney staff have their first name on their name badges as Walt hated being called Mr Disney.

The most popular merchandise item sold at Disneyland theme parks are Mickey's ears.

Lost items at Disney World include millions of pairs of glasses, thousands of mobile phones, digital cameras and hats.

Have a good week my friend. Big Hugs, Antony

Week 24 - The Kindest Humans
Hello Roy,

Kindness is the topic this week. Kindness is a way of thinking, emotional empathy and behaviours. A kind person is often considered to be selfless, friendly, caring, empathetic and compassionate towards others.

World Kindness Day is an annual event celebrated on the 13th November. Its objective is to highlight how human beings can connect through the universal characteristic of kindness, rather than focusing on the differences.

The problem with kindness, is that no person can be kind at all times. It should also be noted that we judge the kindness of others by what they say and do.

But the kindest humans on my list have done more good than bad towards others. Here's the list:

Mother Teresa is the only famous Nun I know. Well apart from the fictional character Deloris Van Cartier (played by Whoopi Goldberg) in *Sister Act*. But I didn't know anything about Mother Teresa until I did some research for this email.

First Mother Teresa was a Roman Catholic Nun. Teresa cared for the sick, including those who suffered from stigma (at the time) as a result of their diseases. This included people with HIV/AIDS, Leprosy and TB. She helped out in food kitchens for the poor, mobile health clinics and counselling programmes.

Unfortunately Mother Teresa was not always kind. Teresa was criticised for her views about contraception and abortion. It was also reported that the environment and care in the hospice she set up were not good.

Florence Nightingale is known as the founder of modern Nursing. She is obviously kind to care for the ill. But what makes her remarkable to me is that she was interested in data analysis. Using data she significantly reduced mortality rates by introducing hand washing (which wasn't common practice in healthcare settings at the time).

Joseph Lister was a British Surgeon who transformed surgery in healthcare by introducing antiseptic techniques during surgery that significantly reduced the mortality rate. He was said to be tireless in his work of improving patient safety and patient outcomes. If this is not kindness, I'm not sure what is.

Mary Seacole is another Nurse, particularly famous for setting up a field hospital to care for soldiers during the Crimean War. Florence Nightingale also had a field hospital in the Crimean War but hers was 100 miles away from the battlefield. Mary's field hospital was much closer to the fighting and it is even reported that on occasion she would go on the battlefield itself to care for and comfort dying soldiers.

Jonas Salk was a superb man who developed the polio vaccination after being deeply impacted by seeing people suffering with polio. He worked on the vaccine for a solid seven years. Jonas also didn't patent the vaccine, stating it belonged to the people. The patient would have been worth $7 billion and therefore would have made Jonas incredibly wealthy.

Today, polio is extremely rare due to the vaccination programmes around the world. But none of it would have been possible without Jonas' vaccine.

Bill and Melinda Gates set up the Bill & Melinda Gates Foundation in 1994. Bill made his money through setting up Microsoft. They set up the foundation to support their Philanthropic efforts. The organisation has spent tens of billions of pounds to provide life-saving medical care. It has also provided computers to help educate children and give them skills that they will need to get on in life.

Oprah Winfrey is many things to many people; including: TV Presenter/Producer, Author, Actress and Businesswoman. Oprah has donated millions of dollars towards children's education and has her own Foundation.

During the COVID-19 outbreak in the United States of America she continued her philanthropic work, providing a food programme for those affected by the pandemic in Chicago, Milwaukee, Nashville, Baltimore and Kosciusko and Mississippi.

Abdul Sattar Edhi is a humanitarian from Pakistan with his kind works taking place in his country of origin. He set up the Edhi Foundation, which runs the largest ambulance network in the world, homeless shelters, rehabilitation shelters, orphanages and animal shelters.

Abdul sadly died in 2016, but had a massive impact on the people in Pakistan. His kindness seemed to know no bounds.

J.K. Rowling is most famous for her captivating wizarding world that she created in the Harry Potter book series. J.K. Rowling has admitted in previous interviews that when she first started her charity efforts she really didn't have an idea about how to go about it and described her efforts as "sporadic."

But then she found her cause and set up the Lumos Foundation. Lumos aims to shut down institutional orphanages and instead support children and their families in the communities in which they live. The work started in 2004 and continues to this day.

My Very Best Wishes,

Antony

Royal Navy Fact:

The Royal Marines are known across the world as one of the most highly trained and elite fighting forces. These 'Commandos' have a history that goes back well over 350 years.

Week 25 - A List of Cakes
Hey Roy,

You know I love cake, right? Well here's a list of cakes, with accompanying descriptions:

- Pumpkin Pie - A sweet pie made from pumpkin pulp and sugar.
- Sticky Toffee Pudding - A moist cake covered in a toffee sauce.
- Banana Bread - Made from bananas that are going off, with plenty of sugar. This is an amazing cake.
- Fairy Cakes - Small individual cakes, come in a variety of styles and flavours.
- Butterfly Cakes - A variant of a fairy cake with buttercream in the centre and two little wings on top of the buttercream that give an appearance of a butterfly, hence the name.
- Rock Cakes - A small cake with a rough surface resembling a rock. My mum makes an incredible rock cake. Her's has a rough service, but soft and bouncy cake filling. Perfection.
- Egg Custards - A yellow desert with a pastry base and sweet egg filing.
- Jaffa Cakes - I would argue these are more of a biscuit. They are made by McVites (as well as own brand imitations) in the UK. They have a sponge base with a smaller orange flavoured circle on top and covered in a layer of milk chocolate.
- Chocolate Eclairs - Two pieces of choux pastry, with fresh cream in the centre and topped with chocolate. They also come as a bun.
- Red Velvet - Sponge cake that has been dyed red with food colouring. Somehow it tastes greatly better than sponge cake.
- Vanilla Slice - Two pieces of flaky pastry with vanilla flavoured custard and topped with white icing.
- Angel Cake - A sponge loaf in the colours of pink, yellow and white. Sandwiched together with buttercream. Mr Kipling's are the best I've tasted so far.
- Chocolate Cake - A cake made of chocolate flavouring.
- Caterpillar Cake - A variation of the chocolate cake above, but in the shape of a caterpillar and with a face.
- Coffee Cake - A cake that is usually served with coffee.

- Walnut Cake - A cake topped with walnuts.
- Rainbow Cake - I've never had this type of cake, but have always wanted one. Each layer is a different colour of the rainbow in the right order.
- Victoria Sponge - A British classic.
- Biscoff cake - A cake made out of Biscoff biscuits.
- Cupcake - An American version of fairy cakes. Slightly bigger than fairy cakes. Sometimes known as a muffin. Come in a variety of styles and flavours.
- Rice Pudding - A sweet pudding made from rice.
- Yule Log - A chocolate cake, with a chocolate topping in the shape of a log. Usually sold at Christmas time.
- Custard - A sweet yellow liquid. Whilst not technically a cake it is usually served with a cake.
- Trifle - A multiple layered cake: sponge, fresh cream and jelly/fruit.
- Carrot Cake - A sweet cake made from carrots and sugar.
- Madeira cake - A denser version of the sponge cake.
- Scones - Small individual bun type cake. Usually cut in half and covered with jam or butter.
- Cheesecake (various flavours) - A cake in the shape and size of a pie. Usually with a biscuit base. Comes in a variety of flavours.
- Black Forest Gateau - A chocolate cake with cherries.
- Apple Pie - A sweet pie made with apples.
- Eccles Cake - A small pastry cake with currants. Originally made in a town called Eccles in Northern England.
- Manchester Tart - A shortcrust pastry shell, spread with raspberry jam, covered with a custard filling and topped with flakes of coconut and a cherry. Named after the location of its invention, Manchester, Northern England.
- Flapjacks - Rectangle made from oats and golden syrup.
- Fondant Fancy - A small sponge cake covered in fondant icing.
- Twinkie - An American cake that was made famous in the film *Zombieland*.

There's very few cakes that I don't like, however one of them is Lemon Drizzle cake. I only really like lemon as a slice in my glass of Pepsi Max.

Another dislike of mine is the Battenberg cake, it's the marzipan coating I don't like on it.

Christmas Cake I have tried and don't like the texture or taste of it.

Tiramisu I will admit I have never tried but don't like the look or name of the cake.

The Bakewell Tart is a cake I've never tried. More than willing to give it a go though.

We simply must go out for coffee and cake on your next annual leave visit. We have lots to catch up on and I can think of no better way of doing it.

Hopefully See You Soon,

Antony

Royal Navy Story:

At the start of World War 1, the German navy had cruiser ships in oceans across the world. They immediately began targeting Allied merchant ships. Their aim was to disrupt supply routes, limiting supplies and damaging the enemy's economy. The Royal Navy was tasked with eliminating as many of these ships as possible.

Later in the war, the Royal Navy used the same strategy that the Germans had used. The Royal Navy began a blockade to restrict supplies to the Germans and their armies. This blockade, which took place over 6 years is often cited as a reason for Britain winning the war.

This wasn't the only action the Royal Navy took. It also mined parts of oceans, closing sections of the oceans off to all ships.

Week 26 - Dark Jokes

Hey Sailor,

This week I have found you some of the darkest jokes on the web. So take a seat and be prepared to be shocked and laugh at the same time:

I was digging in our garden and found a chest full of gold coins. I wanted to run straight home to tell my husband about it. Then I remembered why I was digging in our garden.

Even people who are good for nothing have the capacity to bring a smile to your face, like when you push them down the stairs.

What does my dad have in common with Nemo? They both can't be found.

My husband left a note on the fridge that said, "This isn't working." I'm not sure what he's talking about. I opened the fridge door and it's working fine!

I have many jokes about unemployed people—sadly none of them work.

I made a website for orphans. Unfortunately it doesn't have a home page.

The other day, my girlfriend asked me to pass her lipstick but I accidentally passed her a glue stick. She still isn't talking to me.

What do you call a dog with no legs? It doesn't matter what you call him, he won't come anyway.

My older relatives liked to tease me at weddings, saying things like, "You'll be next!" They stopped once I started doing the same to them at funerals.

My boss told me to have a good day. So I went home.

What did the asteroid that killed the dinosaurs say?

"T-Rex, I'm coming for my hug!"

Patient: "Oh doctor, I'm just so nervous. This is my first operation."
Doctor: "Don't worry. Mine too."

As I get older, I remember all the people I lost along the way. Maybe my budding career as a Tour Guide was not the right choice.

I hope these made you smile at the very least. But I was totally aiming for belly laughter.

Best Wishes,

Antony

Royal Navy Fact:

The Royal Navy fleet is expanding. Currently there are long term plans to add additional ships to the ones already in service.

Week 27 - Why Do People Hoard?
Hi Roy,

Stuff. We all buy and hang on to things for too long. But I once saw this documentary on TV about hoarders. People who literally spent all their time collecting things and storing them in every nook and cranny in their homes (and even in their gardens).

This documentary showed how this one man had a tiny space in what was once his living room in which to eat, sleep and live due to his hoarding.

Upstairs rooms were full from floor to ceiling, with what was essentially rubbish that had been thrown out by others. He couldn't get into the kitchen to cook, or the bathrooms to use the toilet/undertake personal hygiene.

Yet he couldn't stand the thought of getting rid of anything he had collected. Even though the Council had ordered him to do so, as it was a breach of his tenancy agreement, essentially unsafe for him and potentially a public health issue to his community.

The documentary presenter suggested to the man that he get rid of some of the rubbish. When they said this to him, he looked traumatised at just the idea and began to well up. It was clear that this thought had triggered a strong emotional response in this man.

The idea of hoarding has always fascinated me. But I didn't actually know much about it until doing research for this email. So let me share with you, what I have learned:

- Hoarding is a mental illness. It's identified by excessive amounts of disorganised clutter that serves no purpose, but that the person has a deep emotional connection to. It impairs the activities of daily living and can have a massive impact on social relationships.

- The reasons why people hoard are complex. They may have an underlying other mental health illness such as depression, OCD, anxiety or some other psychotic disorder. For some people it is past emotional traumas that cause them to hoard.

- A common theme among people that hoard is that they often have a strong belief about the things they collect. For example, they may feel that they may need the objects they have collected some day or that having a particular object will make them happy.

- Items that a person may hoard may include: newspapers and magazines, clothes, letters (both opened and unopened), plastic bags/cardboard boxes and household supplies. Some people may also collect animals, often many in number and whom they can't look after properly.

- People who hoard may neglect their own self-care because of it. They may not eat/drink, sleep well, complete basic hygiene needs and in some cases be unable to get to and use the toilet regularly.

- The treatment for hoarding in the UK is a referral to the person's local community Mental Health Team who will offer counselling and Cognitive Behavioural Therapy.

Take Care,

Antony

Royal Navy Fact:

The Royal Navy has its own Doctors, Nurses, Dentists, Chefs, Police, Teachers, Firefighters, Human Resources Teams, Scientists and Engineers. These staff are civilians.

Week 28 - Tips to Deal with Loss
Hey Roy,

I hope this email finds you well. It might seem odd to write you an email about how to deal with loss. But we both know that working in the Armed Forces comes with an increased risk of experiencing more loss than the average citizen.

We all have to deal with loss, usually through the death of a loved one. But feelings of loss are not just related to bereavements. We can also feel that same sense of loss if friendships break down, or we lose special opportunities or sentimental objects.

Feelings of loss are difficult to experience, let alone deal with. There's an array of emotions: sadness, anger, denial, shock, guilt, tiredness and feeling overwhelmed.

Grief is the emotional process we go through in dealing with loss. To deal with loss, we must understand grief.

In 1969, Kübler-Ross wrote a book titled *On Death and Dying*. In this book she proposed that grief had five distinct stages: Denial, Anger, Bargaining, Depression and Acceptance.

As you know, in my day job I'm a Nurse and like you I've also experienced loss. I think Kübler-Ross' work is excellent, but I would add:
- The denial stage could also be the stock stage, in the case of sudden and unexpected loss.
- That the stages aren't linear, people can go forwards and backwards through the stages. They can skip stages. All the stages can be experienced in one day, over days, weeks, months or years.
- There's no time limit on grief. Emotional pain takes months or years to recover from.
- We never really fully get over losing someone we love. But they live on in our thoughts, hearts and memories.

Here's some tips for dealing with loss:

- **Talk.**
  Speak about your loss and how you are feeling to family, friends or a professional counsellor.

- **Don't be hard on yourself.**
  Remember that recovering from loss takes time. Don't be hard on yourself or feel guilty for taking the time you need to heal.

- **Remember that a loss can affect your sleep, appetite and energy levels.**
  Be kind to yourself, don't put yourself under too much pressure to get things done. Be aware of your self-care and make sure you keep doing the essential things to keep you in a good state of wellbeing.

- **Do try to maintain a healthy diet and drink plenty of fluids.**
  Your body is like a machine, it can only run on the fuel you give it.

- **Don't drink alcohol to avoid your thoughts and feelings.**
  Apart from possibly having a hangover the next day, alcohol is a depressant drug that will make you feel worse.

- **Stop the blame.**
  Blame leads to a cycle of guilt and shame. The emotions increase your stress levels and will make you feel worse. Remember: What's done is done. No amount of blaming yourself will change this fact.

- **If your loss is a loved one, remember the good times with them.**
  Don't lose focus on them as a person, by focusing on the fact they've died. Remember the good times, the happiness, the joy and the laughter.

Best Wishes,

Antony

Royal Navy Story:

The Falklands War started on 2nd April 1982. Argentina had long wanted the Falklands and two other nearby islands. Argentina had expressed the view that these islands should be under their law and jurisdiction.

On the first day, Argentina invaded and occupied the Falklands. But these islands were British dependent territories. Argentina had assumed that Britain wouldn't go to war to liberate these British territories. But they were mistaken.

Margaret Thatcher, Prime Minister at the time, took quick action. Thatcher instructed the Royal Navy and Airforce to take the islands back. The Royal Navy sent a fleet to engage with the Argentina navy.

The Royal Navy and Airforce were successful in retaking the Falklands, after a 74 day conflict. But no war or conflict is without the human cost paid in lives. In total, 649 Argentine military personnel, 255 British military personnel and 3 Falkland Islanders were killed during the war.

The vast majority of Falkland Islanders consider themselves to be British and are descended from Britain. At the time and even today the opinion of Falkland Islanders is that they want to be part of Britain and not Argentina.

Overall the Royal Navy could count this war as successful. I write this for these reasons: First, it was a relatively short war, it could have gone on for a lot longer. Second, the deaths of military personnel for Britain were lower than that of the deaths of the military personnel of Argentina. This suggests good strategic planning and implementation of operations. Thirdly the civilian casualties were extremely low, considering other historic wars.

Week 29 - What To Do if You Meet a Dolphin
Ahoy Roy,

How are you my dear friend? I've lost track of how long you've been on deployment now. I hope you are still enjoying your time aboard ship and that above all you are safe.

Dolphins are fascinating creatures. According to some they are more intelligent than us, highly social, playful and adaptable. They are an animal I would love to see and interact with.

Dolphins live in waters all around the world, so at some point you might get to see and even interact with these marvellous animals.

So what to do if you meet a Dolphin:

1. **Introduce yourself.**
   Introduce yourself to the Dolphin, no need to include your rank. The Dolphin will respond with a unique whistle, which is how Dolphins identify one another.

2. **Pay them a compliment.**
   We all love compliments, right? Pay the Dolphin a compliment. I wouldn't mention the lack of hair. I'd probably say something like: "Oh, nice eyes. And I just love your skin."

3. **Tell them a joke.**
   Dolphin's always seem to be quite humorous. So try telling the Dolphin a joke to build rapport.

4. **Play a game with the Dolphin.**
   Dolphin's just love to play games. So come up with a game and play it with the Dolphin. Just remember - no kicking type games (the Dolphin doesn't have any legs) or contact sports (the Dolphin might take them as a sign of aggression). Oh and be sure to let the Dolphin win.

5. **Invite the Dolphin to dinner.**
   Dolphin's like to eat fish whole and head first to prevent the fish's spine from hurting the Dolphin's throat. So no *Nandos, McDonalds, Burger King,* or other fast food restaurants.

6. **Meet the Dolphin's family.**
   Dolphin's families are called pods and the Dolphin's pod can be any size between 2-15 dolphins. Don't forget to say hi to the Dolphin's Aunt Phillis.

7. **Say thank you, exchange numbers and keep in touch.**
   Hopefully by now you've got over the language barrier with the Dolphin. Dolphin's communicate by whistles, clicks and by making other sounds. So say goodbye, exchange numbers (if the Dolphin has a waterproof mobile) and keep in regular contact with your new friend.

Write Soon,

Antony

Royal Navy Fact:

In 2013 a report suggested the Royal Navy is too small. The report suggested that if Britain were attacked, we would have to rely on support from allies.

This is concerning, as Britain is an independent island nation. Being a separate island from central Europe, the Royal Navy has proven itself as essential for the defence of Britain countless times in the past.

Week 30 - Manners
Hey Roy,

My mother always says: "Manners cost nothing." And it's true isn't it?

In British culture, manners and social etiquette are highly valued for showing respect and sometimes gratitude to others. Manners are about more than saying Please and Thank You.

There's a whole list of different British manners to be polite, rules which apply under different circumstances.

1. **Table Manners -** There's a whole list of rules for eating, including: no elbows on the table, no eating or talking with your mouthful, place your serviette on your knees, never reach across the table if you can't reach something - ask someone to pass the food to you.

2. **Being on Time -** This is a weird one. Some people consider being late to be rude, but not all. Some of my friends are regularly late, to the point where I've come to expect it. They are not meaning to be rude, they're just bad at time keeping.

3. **Paying for Drinks in the Pub -** If drinking in rounds at a pub, it is considered rude for someone not to buy a round for everyone. Or to order an overly expensive drink on somebody else's round.

4. **Holding the Door Open for Someone -** If you're coming through a door and there is somebody behind you, it is considered polite to hold the door open for them.

5. **Apologising -** Saying sorry is considered polite if you have said or done something wrong. But the apology must come across as genuine to the person you are apologising to.

6. **Talking or Asking About the Weather -** It's *very* British when making small talk to make comments on or ask about the weather. Nobody knows why! We just do.

One final thing to note about manners: they are different everywhere. So Roy, as you travel the world be aware of your manners and you'll go far.

Big Hugs,

Antony

Royal Navy Story:

Rear Admiral Horatio Nelson was around during the Napoleonic Wars. Nelson is credited with a number of Royal Navy victories against the French navy.

The most significant of Nelson's successes came in 1798. The French had a plan to take what was known as 'British India' at the time. The French planned to do this via Egypt.

Nelson's fleet caught up with the French fleet at Aboukir Bay, near the Rosetta entrance to the Nile. The French had failed to plan to defend their fleet while anchored. Nelson took this opportunity and his attack was an outstanding success.

During the battle, it is estimated that 2,000-3,000 French sailors died, whereas about 218 British sailors died. Nelson's fleet sank 13 French ships without losing a single ship.

Week 31 - 13 Weird Body Facts

Hi Roy,

There's some really weird facts about the human body. Some facts that make me think: *What the heck?* Let me share 13 of these with you:

1. On a man, the ears, nose and prostate continue growing throughout his life. This doesn't improve hearing, sense of smell or improve fertility.

2. Cancers are all caused by the body's cells mutating during the duplication process.

3. The human body has two of some organs (like the lungs and kidneys). The weird fact is that someone can survive if only one of the organs is functioning. For example, some people live with only one functioning lung or kidney.

4. The human mouth can't eat and breathe at the same time.

5. The acid in the stomach is so strong that it can dissolve metal.

6. The gut (small and large intestine) are linked directly to the brain. This discovery explains why food digestion can be impacted by things like depression, anxiety and stress.

7. A male body produces approximately 500 billion sperm cells in the average lifespan. However some men with fertility issues will produce less.

8. In all male bodies not all sperm cells are duplicated correctly, meaning there are defective sperm cells produced.

9. Sperm can live in a body (women's or men's) for 5-7 days. Whereas a female's ovum only lives for 1 day.

10. In a female body the menopause generally starts around 45-55 years old. During menopause although the risk of pregnancy is low, it can happen.

11. The oldest female body to give birth to a baby was 66 years old.

12. The brain's capacity for storing information is said to be "unlimited." This fact goes no way to explaining my poor memory.

13. The human body releases a small amount of light. The eyes of bodies aren't sensitive enough to see this light, but it is detectable through medical machinery. I *wonder* what the purpose of this light is?

Best Wishes,

Antony

Royal Navy Fact:

In World War 2, Winston Churchill, Prime Minister of the time, instructed the Royal Navy to rescue and evacuate Allied soldiers from Dunkirk, France after the German army had surrounded them by land. The Royal Navy successfully saved more than 338,000 Allied soldiers.

Week 32 - Bottom Humour
Ahoy Roy the Sailor,

The aim of this email is to make you laugh with some good old jokes about bottoms. So I've searched the internet and this is the best out of what I found:

Why did the toilet roll down the hill?
It wanted to get to the bottom!

What's got the biggest bum in the world?
The bottom of the ocean.

What has two butts and kills people?
An assassin.

If you slap Dwayne Johnson's butt...
You officially hit rock bottom.

Why did Buddha start pulling coins out of his butt?
"Because change comes from within."

A group of butts is walking. The smallest struggles to keep up.
It says: "Sorry, I'm a little behind."

My boyfriend gave me a butt massage today, but only focused on one cheek. It was very half-assed.

A man was hospitalised with 6 plastic horses up his butt. The doctors described his condition as stable.

Did you hear how Thor saved Loki's butt? With an Asgard.

To be honest, I thought there'd be more decent bottom jokes than this. But these were the only okay-ish ones on the web.

Until Next Week,

Antony

Week 33 - 10 Ways to Be More Creative
Hello My Dear Friend,

We are all creative beings. In your current role, I know you'll be using your creativity everyday to solve problems. Creativity has several benefits including:
- Creativity helps you 'think outside the box' and come up with better solutions to problems.
- Creativity reduces stress levels, so is good for your physical and mental health.
- Creativity encourages collaboration with others and promotes team working.
- Creativity increases team morale.
- Creativity enables you to change patterns of behaviour that no longer benefit or serve you.

Here's 10 ways to be more creative:
1. **Try New Things.**
   This helps your brain to grow new neural pathways and therefore think in new and different ways.

2. **Keep a Diary or Journal.**
   Reflecting on experiences is a great way for you to learn and imagine how you could have handled situations differently. It helps prepare you for similar experiences in the future.

3. **Give Yourself Realistic Deadlines.**
   Deadlines bring a sense of urgency to a problem or puzzle. People often find that deadlines help them come up with solutions quicker.

4. **Take Opportunities to Talk and Do with Others.**
   This gives you the opportunity to collaborate. Others may come up with different ways of doing things, by looking at problems or puzzles from their own unique perspectives.

5. **Listen to Music.**
   Music helps stimulate different parts of your brain and can help you think differently.

6. **Relax - Go Exercise or Go for a Shower.**
   Take some time to relax and distract yourself from the problem or puzzle. Later on, when looking at the problem or puzzle to find solutions your brain is working from a place of being calm and collected.

7. **Take a Break - Go Make a Drink or Go Make a Snack.**
   Similar to the last one: your brain will be calm and collected. But not only that, you're also keeping your body and brain in optimum health by providing essential fuel.

8. **Take a Quick Nap.**
   Sleep, even a short nap, helps refresh and recharge your mind.

9. **Challenge Your Mind Regularly with Puzzles and Brain Teasers.**
   Word searches, crosswords, sudoku and brain teasers all help stretch the limits of your mind. Exercising your brain in this way will stretch your thinking capacity. It is essential to do this regularly, like physical exercise to get the best results.

10. **Read about Creativity and Innovation.**
    Reading is a brilliant way to expand your mind. An expanded mind means more ideas are generated.

Best Wishes,

Antony

Royal Navy Fact:

The Royal Navy stops illicit substances from entering the UK. A 2022 report stated that over 11 metric tonnes of illicit substances have been stopped from entering the UK.

Week 34 - Stress: What It Is & How To Beat It
Hi Roy,

How are you today?

Stress is defined as a body's response to thoughts, emotions or situations that make the person or animal feel under pressure. Short term stress gets the human's or animal's body ready to fight, flight or freeze. It is part of the brain's survival system.

But long term stress or chronic stress can be damaging to physical and mental health.

Stress lowers the immune system's response and puts the body at higher risks of a range of long term diseases such as cardiovascular disease. Stress increases the risk of developing mental illnesses including anxiety and depression.

There isn't a specific blood test to diagnose stress. It is usually diagnosed by a Doctor asking about symptoms. Symptoms of stress include:

Physical Symptoms	**Mental Symptoms**	**Behaviours**
• Headaches. • Insomnia. • Stomach or digestive complaints. • Muscle tension or pain. • Chest pain / palpitations. • Reduced interest in sex. • Panic attacks.	• Worrying. • Feeling angry or getting easily frustrated. • Feeling overwhelmed. • Racing thoughts. • Loss of interest in everyday activities.	• Difficulty focusing, solving tasks and thinking things through. • Jaw clenching. • Crying or feeling like you might. • Snapping at people.

We all experience stress at times. But the great thing about you serving in the Royal Navy - is that you will already do the below, which are proven strategies for managing stress:

- Keep a routine.
- Eat a balanced diet and drink plenty of fluids.
- Get enough rest and sleep.
- Stay active - exercise regularly.
- Connect with others. Talking helps reduce stress levels and your peers may be able to support you.
- Be aware of things that trigger a stress response in you.
- Set realistic and achievable goals.
- Saying no to taking on additional work or tasks when you're already stressed.

Take Care My Friend,

Antony

Royal Navy Fact:

The main task of the Royal Navy in the Cold War was to find Russian submarines, as these were the biggest threat to other naval units.

Week 35 - Will AI Robots Take Over The World?

Hey Roy,

There's a lot of talk at home right now about Artificial Intelligence (AI) and the impact that it might have in society in the near future. We both remember the *Terminator* films and the famous catch phrase: *I'll be back!*

AI is a worry for some. People who do low skilled monotonous jobs could be out of a job. For example, computers can already listen to videos and audio and translate words spoken into written text. This means that the one time essential roles in businesses of Secretaries and Note Takers are no longer necessary.

Add a bit of intelligence to this and jobs like Data Analyst, Call Centre Workers, Taxi Drivers, Bookkeepers, Editors/Reporters and even Graphic Designers could be a thing of the past for humans.

Now let's talk about robots. Most are not even close to being as versatile and flexible as a human body is. There would probably need to be significant developments in the design and mass production of these robots for them to risk taking people's jobs. Let alone taking over the world.

I think the fundamental reason AI won't take over the world is because we've all seen the *Terminator* and other similar films. As humans, I don't think we'd fully trust clever technology with anything truly important to us.

Write Soon,

Antony

Royal Navy Fact:

The Naval Defence Act (1859) required the Royal Navy to maintain a high enough number of battleships to be able to defeat in combat the next two largest navies in the world combined.

My Royal Navy Friend

Week 36 - 20 Super Space Facts
Hi Roy,

Space. It's big, it's black and full of shiny stars. Here are 20 super space facts:

1. The universe is still expanding and has been doing so since its birth - the Big Bang.

2. There are more stars in the universe, than there are grains of sand making up every beach on Earth.

3. Black holes absorb all forms of matter. It is theorised that at least one black hole exists at the centre of most galaxies. There is one at the centre of our galaxy, the Milky Way. Apparently it's travelling towards the Earth, but it has plenty of distance to cover before it reaches our solar system.

4. Nebulas are a collection of gases and dust in space that are being pulled together slowly by gravity. They are fascinating because not only do they admit light and colours (due to ionised gases); but they can also serve as interstellar nurseries.

5. Space is very cold at −270.45 °C.

6. Water is everywhere! Scientists used to think that in our solar system, water only existed on Earth. Scientists now have strong evidence that there is water on Mercury, Mars, Jupiter, Saturn, Uranus and Neptune.

7. A massive asteroid is theorised to have wiped out all land-based dinosaurs. The asteroid is likely to have been made out of clay, silicate rocks and nickel-iron.

8. The Andromeda Galaxy is approaching ours at a rate 68 miles per second. When they collide they will create something new - an elliptical galaxy.

9. Our sun is of average size. It takes up 99.86% of our solar system.

10. There are currently over 4,000 Earth-like planets that we know of which might support life.

11. Shooting stars are space debris that burn up when they enter Earth's atmosphere.

12. Nobody knows who first gave the Earth its name.

13. It is theorised that there are white holes. They spew out matter, doing the opposite to what black holes do. However, we are yet to discover one of these white holes.

14. It takes light from the sun 8 minutes and 20 seconds to reach our eyes on planet Earth.

15. In 2016, scientists detected a radio signal from a source 5 billion light-years away. When this radio signal was sent the Earth didn't even exist yet.

16. On Venus the rain is made from sulfuric acid.

17. Laika from Russia was the first dog to go to space.

18. Diamonds are found throughout our galaxy and the universe. Theoretically there is also a diamond planet out there that is made completely or mostly out of diamonds.

19. There are already over half a million pieces of rubbish orbiting the Earth thanks to mankind. Hopefully most will be destroyed by falling into the atmosphere.

20. Space is vast. All the stars, planets and galaxies would only make up about 4% of the universe. The rest is darkness - dark space and dark matter.

Write Soon,

Antony

Royal Navy Fact:

The Royal Navy has been fighting pirates throughout its history. The latest pirate interaction was in 2008, when Somali pirates tried to take a civilian vessel and the Royal Navy were forced to intervene.

Week 37 - Bar Jokes
Hello My Friend,

How are you today? We all love a good bar joke. My absolutely favourite joke of all-time is the cheesy classic:

>A horse walks into a bar.
>The Bar Man says: "Why the long face?"

But I'm sure there's better bar jokes out there. So I went in search of the best bar jokes online. Here's what I found:

The past, present, and future walk into a bar.
It was tense.

Comic Sans, Helvetica, and Times New Roman walk into a bar. "Get out!" shouts the bartender. "We don't serve your type!"

A man walks into a bar and orders a drink.
A minute later he hears, "You look great. Have you lost weight?"
He looks around, but there's no one near.
Again, a minute later, he hears, "You know, you don't look a day over thirty."
Looks around again, no one but him and the bartender, so he asks, "Did you hear that?"
The bartender says, "It's the peanuts. They're complimentary."

A man walks into a bar. He said, "Ouch, that hurt."

A crab walks into a bar and says, "I'll have a pint please, but if I'm not satisfied with it, I'd like to be compensated with 10 bottles of champagne."
The bartender says, "Why the big clause?"

A ghost walks into a bar and the bartender says, "Sorry, we don't serve spirits."

A polar bear walks into a bar and says to the bartender: "I'll have a Gin and... Tonic."
The bartender asks, "Why the big pause?"
The polar bear replies, "I don't know, I've always had them."

A sandwich walks into a bar.
The Bartender says, "Sorry sir, we don't serve food here."

A skeleton walks into a bar and says, "Gimme a pint and a mop."

George R.R. Martin, Joss Whedon, and Steven Moffat walk into a bar, and everyone you've ever loved dies.

A snake walks into a bar.
The bartender says, "How the hell did you do that?"

A penguin walks into a bar and asks the barman, "Has my brother been in for a drink here today?"
The bartender looks at the penguin and says, "I'm not sure. What does he look like?"

I was in the pub when a guy called me a cheapskate. So I threw his drink in his face.

I'm not saying my local pub is rough...but the first prize at the pub quiz was two weeks' alibi.

After a heavy night at the pub, I was rudely awakened by my neighbour cutting his grass. Sod it I thought, he can mow around me.

Best Wishes,

Antony

Royal Navy Fact:

The HMS Protector has a unique role in the Royal Navy. It patrols the Antarctic and its role is to provide support to the British Antarctic Survey (BAS).

Week 38 - Famous Film Quotes
Hi Roy,

Whenever I think of a famous quote from films, it is always:

Show me the money! - Jerry Maguire (1996)

But there are many famous film quotes. So here's a short list of some of my favourites:

Just keep swimming. - Finding Nemo (2003)

Roads? Where we're going we don't need roads.
- Back to the Future (1985)

That'll do, pig. That'll do.
- Babe (1995)

Nobody puts Baby in a corner. - Dirty Dancing (1987)

They may take our lives, but they'll never take our freedom!
- Braveheart (1995)

May the Force be with you. - Star Wars (1977)

I feel the need — the need for speed! - Top Gun (1986)

You've got red on you. - Shaun of the Dead (2004)

Keep your friends close, but your enemies closer.
- The Godfather Part II (1974)

I am Groot. - Guardians of the Galaxy (2014)

E.T. phone home. - E.T. The Extra-Terrestrial (1982)

I wish I knew how to quit you. - Brokeback Mountain (2005)

I see you. - Avatar (2009)

My Royal Navy Friend

What I'm trying to say, very inarticulately, is that, um, in fact, perhaps despite appearances, I like you, very much. Just as you are.
- Bridget Jones's Diary (2001)

Even the smallest person can change the course of the future.
- The Lord of the Rings: The Fellowship of the Ring (2001)

Your scientists were so preoccupied with whether or not they could, they didn't stop to think if they should.
- Jurassic Park (1993)

Don't be careless, but don't be too careful either.
D3: The Mighty Ducks (1996)

There's no place like home. - The Wizard of Oz (1939)

Don't dream it. Be it. - The Rocky Horror Picture Show (1975)

I'll be back. - The Terminator (1984)

Until Next Week,

Antony

Royal Navy Fact:

About 1,000 ships made up the Royal Navy in 1859. This included both combat and support vessels.

Week 39 - 9 Travel Tips

Hello My Friend,

One of the many advantages of your career in the Royal Navy, is that it brings with it the opportunity to travel. So here's some good travel tips:

1. Do your research - find out things to see and do and make an itinerary, to make sure you fit everything in.

2. Check the recommendations for vaccinations and treatments prior to travelling and get these done.

3. Know the currency, language and cultural norms of the place you're planning to visit.

4. Make sure people know your travel plans for safety reasons.

5. Make sure you have travel insurance or can access healthcare in an emergency.

6. Take travel plugs, power banks and charger leads for your essential electronic devices.

7. Take any prescribed medications with you when you travel.

8. Carry cash, bank cards, passport, mobile phone and other essentials with you at all times.

9. In some places - don't drink the water. Only drink bottled water, or you may get ill.

Best Wishes,

Antony

Week 40 - Ancient Egyptian Curses
Hey Roy,

The ancient Egyptians weren't against throwing a curse on anyone who would interfere with their dead.

Perhaps the most famous ancient Egyptian curse is that of the one on Tutankhamun's tomb. The tomb was opened in 1923. The warning on the tomb read:

Death shall approach on rapid wings to him who disrupts the King's tranquillity.

The financial sponsor of the expedition, Lord Carnarvon, died just four months after disturbing Tutankhamun's tomb. Weirdly, he died of a mosquito bite on his cheek, which got infected and led to sepsis. As time has gone by, things have been added to this story. Like the fact that when Lord Carnarvon died, all his lights went out.

Zahi Hawass, an Egyptologist, took items from Kom Abu Billo's tomb. On the day that he removed the items his aunt died. Exactly 1 year after that his uncle died. A year later, his favourite cousin died. Despite these deaths, Hawass denied believing in the curse. Just a coincidence then Hawass? I think not.

An Archaeologist was taking two adult mummies from Bahariya Oasis' tomb to a museum. He started having nightmares about two children. These nightmares didn't stop until the adult mummies were reunited with two child mummies already at the museum.

In 1971, Brian Emery discovered a little statue of Osiris (the Egyptian God of Death) near the small village of Sakkara, Egypt. Emery took the statue home. Emery was later found with right-sided paralysis and was unable to communicate. The next day he died.

In 2007, an item stolen from Egypt was returned to the Egyptian Embassy in Germany. An anonymous handwritten note explained that the person's father had stolen the item and that it had caused nothing but trouble for the family since. Apparently, the father had developed paralysis and died shortly after returning from Egypt with the item.

My Royal Navy Friend

In 2013 in a Museum in Manchester somethin weird started to happen. A statue on exhibit from an ancient Egyptian tomb rotated 180 degrees every three days. It was in a locked glass cabinet that only the curator had access to.

The mummies body had been destroyed and the curator suggested that this statue could be used as an alternative receptacle for the mummies spirit according to ancient Egyptian beliefs. Scientists set up time lapse cameras and indeed the statue did indeed change position on its own.

Write Soon,

Antony

Royal Navy Fact:

All ex-serving personnel can be called back into the Royal Navy, should there be a time of need.

Week 41 - Things Money Can't Buy
Hi Roy,

Money is unfortunately essential to live. We require it for food, shelter, safety and even in some cases healthcare. But there are some things money can't buy, including:

1. **Time**
   No matter how much money you have, your time alive on this planet will always be limited. Noone knows how much time we have left, so we should always make the most of it.

   That said, we can be clever and use money to help us prioritise our time. For example, my friend employs a cleaner for 5 hours a week, so that he can spend the 5 hours he would have spent cleaning following his passions.

   I can't afford a cleaner, so instead I just keep my cleaning time and activities to a minimum.

2. **Physical, Mental & Emotional Health**
   Money can help access both preventative and disease treatment healthcare. It also means you can eat a better diet, have time to exercise regularly and live in an environment that is better for your health.

   But what money can't do is alter your biology. Your genetic predisposition to good health and diseases.

3. **Loving & Supportive Relationships**
   If you won a large amount of money through the lottery tomorrow, I'm sure you'd acquire a lot of new 'friends.' It is likely that suddenly your love life would take a positive turn. Some family members would be suddenly interested in having a deep and meaningful relationship with you.

   But would these genuine and authentic relationships? Likely not.

   Loving and supportive relationships can't be bought.

4. **Qualities**
   The qualities that make up a person through their thoughts, what they say and do are not for sale. I'm thinking of qualities like kindness, trustworthiness and loyalty.

5. **An (Award Winning) Personality**
   A personality or in my case a self-awarded winning personality can't be bought with cash. A good personality for me includes eccentricity, intelligence and a good dose of humour.

6. **True Happiness**
   Money makes life more comfortable, but it can't make you happy. Happiness is something everyone wants, but it is often elusive.

   That's because happiness is different for everyone. Plus there's no one formula to achieve happiness that works for everyone.

7. **Passion and Enthusiasm for Life**
   Passion, enthusiasm and motivation for life are all wonderful things. But they are definitely things that money can't buy.

8. **Llamacorns, Unicorns and Other Magnificent Mythical Beasts**
   I wish money could buy these things. But these creatures all come from the imagination and that is something you've either got or not.

Write Soon,

Antony

Royal Navy Fact:

The Royal Navy has a long historic association with the Royal Family, hence the name. All young Royals are strongly encouraged to spend some time serving in the Armed Forces to help them to understand the important work that the Armed Forces do.

Week 42 - Whatever Happened to The Roman Empire?
Hello My Friend,

How are you? I hope this email finds you well. One of my favourite things to learn about at school was the Roman Empire. The Roman Empire really did change the world by inventing things like: roads, underfloor heating, cement, sanitation systems and elements of surgical procedures.

But what happened to the Roman Empire? Why did it fall? Experts have different opinions on what ultimately led to the downfall of the Roman Empire. But most agree that there were a range of complex issues including:

- **Economic Issues**
  The empire had decades of overspending on wars, public works and wasteful projects. Tax on citizens was at its highest point. But most importantly the gap between the rich and poor was at its widest. Inequality bred disillusionment for the poor citizens.

  Add to this that as the empire was overly reliant on slave labour. But with no new lands being conquered, no new slaves were coming into the empire and this had a massive economic impact.

- **Lack of Military Strength & Coordination**
  The empire was once famous for the strength and coordination of its military. But towards the end, there were countless military defeats and enemies on several borders. This suggests the military lacked strength, coordination and a comprehensive strategy.

- **Precarious Politics**
  The empire had several political leaders in a short space of time, each with a different idea with how the empire should be managed. Leaders were being murdered, corruption was so present in the Senate that it was widely known by the general populous. Understandably, the people lost trust in their politicians.
- **Religious Tensions**
  Christianity came along, replacing the empire's previous polytheistic religion. This had a major impact on the people's values system. They became less about the glory of the state and more about individual leaders - setting them up as selected by God and more about the church. This change of values and beliefs could not have been implemented at a worse time.

The Roman Empire collapsed and had had its day. But the global impact on the world has stood the test of time and we still see this impact in our daily lives today.

Best Wishes,

Antony

Royal Navy Fact:
You must be between 16 to 39 years old to enlist in the Royal Navy. You must also be physically fit, under a certain weight and above a certain height to enlist.

There are also other conditions that may exclude people from enlisting in the Royal Navy including: criminal history, past or present substance use, certain tattoos or tattoos in certain places on the body and piercings that can't be removed (including flesh tunnels).

There are additional requirements to enlist as a Royal Navy Officer, which includes certain qualifications.

Week 43 - Mood Lifters

Hey Roy,

We all have good and bad days. When you're having a bad day, use these mood lifters to bring your mood back up:

1. **Music** - Put on some upbeat music. Music can instantly put us in a good mood and can be quite motivational.

2. **Food** - Certain foods are classed as mood lifters. These foods include: salad, vegetables, fresh fruit, eggs, ginger, coffee, chocolate and chicken.

3. **Clean** - Cleaning yourself or your environment is known to lift your mood.

4. **Exercise** - Any sort of exercise gives you a hit of endorphins and improves your mood. But you can increase this hit even more by doing team sports with others.

5. **Sleep** - Hit the sack and get a goodnight's sleep.

6. **Spend Time in Nature** - If at all possible, spend time in nature. We're not sure exactly why, but this does seem to put people in a better mood.

7. **Connect with Friends and Family** - If you have time, spend time with your shipmates or give a family member at home a quick call.

8. **Laughter** - A joke or thinking of something you find funny is an instant mood boost.

9. **Consider Meditation** - This isn't an instant mood lifter, but if you practise meditation on a regular basis, research suggests that it does lift mood in the longer term.

Big Hugs,

Antony
Week 44 - Neurodiversity Super Powers
Ahoy Sailor!

Neurodiversity is about recognising that not everybody's brain is wired or operates in the same way. In the past, those with neurodiverse brains were often viewed as being at a distinct disadvantage to the general population.

At one time, people with neurodiverse brains were often considered to be less intelligent than the general population. They were often expected by education institutions to try to adapt their cognition to match that of their peers.

However over time we have learned to value this neurodiversity. We now appreciate the unique neurodiversity of individuals and appreciate their individual strengths, talents and resourcefulness in developing coping strategies.

So what exactly are neurodiverse conditions? Well they include:

- **Attention Deficit Hyperactivity Disorder (ADHD)**

A neurological condition that affects attention and focus. People with ADHD tend to be impulsive and struggle thinking things through before they do them.

I have a number of friends with ADHD and the great thing about them is that I'm never bored. Conversations and activities are always brilliantly fun and often go off on the most random tangents.

A real strength for anyone with ADHD is the ability to hyperfocus, meaning they learn about something new quickly, in great detail and they tend to become experts in whatever they are focused on.

- **Autism**

Autism is different for every person with it. How it impacts them is so unique. But generally people with autism may struggle to communicate with others, understand what others are thinking or feeling, like routines, get stressed out by unfamiliar situations or unexpected events and take longer to process information given.

There are some things that people with autism are particularly good at compared with others without autism. These include tasks involving logic, facts and sometimes mathematical/computer programming type tasks.

- **Dyslexia**

People with dyslexia often struggle to effectively communicate in writing. They struggle to get their ideas on paper. It also affects their ability to read and sometimes comprehend what they read.

People with dyslexia are often very good at verbalising their thoughts, ideas and plans.

Now that there is more emphasis on presenting data in more ways than just writing (think tables, charts, drawings/diagrams, images, videos, etc.), people with dyslexia can use these methods to better communicate with others.

- **Dyscalculia**
  People with dyscalculia struggle with numbers and mathematical calculations. This is probably the least diagnosed neurodiverse condition. Thankfully, calculators and new ways of teaching people about numbers have helped people with dyscalculia.

- **Dyspraxia**
  Is a neurodiverse condition affecting coordination, spatial awareness and balance. People with this neurodiverse condition struggle with physical activities such as sports, dancing and activities requiring good hand-eye coordination.

All of these conditions are on a spectrum and affect individuals to varying degrees.

The great thing about neurodiverse people is their ability to adapt and come up with superb coping strategies to complete tasks effectively.

People can also be diagnosed with more than one of these conditions, which adds additional complexity to neurodiverse people navigating through life.

I'm sure now that you know more about neurodiversity you can understand why we now value it. Some employers are even starting to design jobs and work processes to get the most productivity out of employees who are neurodiverse.

Write Soon,

Antony

Royal Navy Fact:

There is lots of slang language used in the Royal Navy. For example, if someone in the Royal Navy says that they are going to *Gonk*, it means they are going to bed to sleep. If they say something is *hoofing*, they mean it is very good.

Week 45 - 10 Weird Olympic Games
Hi Roy,

This week I thought I'd delight you with some weird categories in the Olympic Games:

1. Pigeon Shooting - I wouldn't really call this one weird, more cruel to the poor pigeons. But back in the 1900s, pigeon shooting was a game. Competitors were eliminated if they missed two pigeons in a row and the winner was the competitor who killed the most pigeons.

2. Pistol Duelling - No actual humans were harmed in this Olympic game. This again was in the 1900s. Instead, competitors shot appropriately dressed mannequins. The mannequins had targets painted on them with scores. The competitor who scored the highest was the winner.

3. Walking - Believe it or not, this was and still is an olympic game. Participants are not allowed to run and must walk in a pre-defined way. Winner is the fastest to the finish line. This is the only Olympic game I could ever see myself taking part in!

4. Poodle Clipping - This again was an Olympic game in the 1900s. It was a test game, but didn't make it to become an official game. The winner was the competitor that could clip the coats of the most poodles in two hours.

5. Obstacle Swim - Again this was a game in the 1900s. It was basically an obstacle course in water. Winner was the quickest to complete the obstacle course. To be honest, I would have liked to have watched this Olympic game.

6. Hot Air Ballooning - It didn't become an official Olympic game, but balloon enthusiasts did try. The plan was to get judges to assess competitors on a range of criteria to decide the winner.

7. Trampoline - Has been an official Olympic game since 2000. I'm not sure what's expected of the competitors or how they decide the winner of this one.

8. Water Skiing - Weirdly only ever appeared as an Olympic game once and never returned.

9. Skateboarding - Yes, it's an official Olympic game.

10. Bowling - Another weird Olympic game. Which apparently is very popular.

Best Wishes,

Antony

Royal Navy Fact:

There aren't many celebrities who've served in the Royal Navy. But business person Duncan Bannatyne (who became a celebrity after being a Dragon on the BBC's Dragon's Den) did serve. That was until he was discharged for throwing an Officer overboard.

My Royal Navy Friend

Week 46 - Some Wonderful Words We Should Use More
Hello My Friend,

I love the variety of the English vocabulary. There are some wonderful words that I don't think we use often enough. Here they are, with their meanings:

- **Abundance** - To have plenty of something.

- **Adore** - Admire or think fondly of.

- **Candour** - To be completely honest.

- **Captivating** - Fascinating, holding your attention.

- **Conundrum** - A difficult problem or puzzle.

- **Cumulative** - The impact builds with the repeated action.

- **Dazzling** - Shining, attracting attention.

- **Diminutive** - An extremely small impact.

- ☐ **Enthralling** - Fascinating or holding your attention.

- ☐ **Fiasco** - A complete disaster.

- ☐ **Glorious** - Wonderful / brilliant / marvellous.

- ☐ **Immense** - Extremely large or great.

- ☐ **Opulent** - Luxurious or expensive.

- ☐ **Savvy** - Clever or knows what they are doing.

- ☐ **Whimsical** - Playful, possibly pointless and always amusing.

Best Wishes,

Antony
Week 47 - How to Teach a Sea Lion to Dance
Hi Roy,

I hope this email finds you well. Sea lions love a good tune and like to dance. But unfortunately sea lions aren't naturally very good dancers.

So should the occasion call for it, you may be required in the Royal Navy to teach a sea lion how to dance. Here's how I'd go about it:

First choose the style of dance. I've heard that sea lions quite like street dance.

Next create a playlist of appropriate music.

Now it's time to choose your dance moves and design a routine to the music. Here's some classic moves:

- ☐ Side-to-side Step
  The classic old people's dance move by stepping from side to side. Think of your Nan dancing at a family party.

My Royal Navy Friend

- [ ] The Moon Walk
  Walking backwards, sometimes with arm movements. Think of Michael Jackon's Thriller music video.

- [ ] The Robot
  Making robotic-like movements with your arms and legs.

- [ ] Spinning
  Making a full 360 degree turn either way.

- [ ] Brushing off Your Shoulders
  Using your hands (or in this case flippers) to brush something imaginary off your shoulders.

- [ ] Jazz Flippers
  Outstretched flippers in a waving motion.

- [ ] The Shoulder Lean
  Lean one shoulder forwards, back and then do the same with the other.

- [ ] Shake Your Backside
  Shake your backside to the rhythm of the song.

- [ ] Run on the Spot
  Pretend to run (or maybe in this case swim?) on the spot.

- [ ] Star Jump
  Jump in the air with your hands and tail stretched out.

- [ ] The Egyptian
  Famous from the song *Walk Like An Egyptian* by The Bangles. Point your hands/flippers outwards at either side of your body and move them forwards and backwards.

- [ ] The YMCA
  Make the shape of the letters YMCA with your body. Made famous by the *YMCA* by The Pet Shop Boys.

- Step Clap
  Step from side to side whilst clapping your hands/flippers.

- The Chicken
  Step from side to side, whilst flapping your arms/flippers up and down like a chicken.

Finally teach your sea lion your dance routine. If they are any good, get them an Talent Agent and send them on Britain's Got Talent to seek fame and fortune.

Big Hugs,

Antony

Week 48 - The Great Emu War of 1932
Hello My Friend,

Did you know that in 1932 the Australian Army went to war with Emus? Only in Australia!

Now known as The Great Emu War, Australian farmers complained to their Government about Emus eating their wheat crops. The farmers said that their crops were being devastated and that the Emu's population was skyrocketing.

The Australian Government responded by sending in the army. Their were some conditions to the deployment including:
- Guns were only to be used by military personnel. Okay, this makes sense for safety reasons.
- Troop transport would be paid for by the Australian Government.
- Farmers would have to provide military personnel with food, accommodation and payment for the bullets used.

In the first conflict, the army spotted around 50 emus. The plan was to herd the emus into an ambush. But the Emus split into smaller groups and ran off. Later that day, a small group of emus were spotted and some were killed.

The army continued with its strategy to ambush large groups of Emus. The army managed to herd more than a thousand emus into a kill zone. But their guns jammed and they only managed to kill twelve emus.

Four days into the campaign the army had had very limited success. Army leaders stated two reasons for this:
1. The weather (it had rained).
2. Emu leaders - Groups of emus had leaders who kept a lookout for danger. These leaders were alerting their groups to the danger posed by the soldiers and the groups were running away.

At this point, the only success the army could claim is that there had been no injuries or deaths of the soldiers. Overall around 500 emus had been killed in this part of the conflict. The Australian Government ordered the withdrawal of the troops.

But the farmers went back to the Australian Government and asked for military intervention again, as the emus were continuing to eat or otherwise damage their crops. The army this time killed around 1,000 emus directly and another 2,500 emus died of wounds from bullets that the soldiers fired.

This conflict ended when a bounty system was introduced. But both sending in the military and the bounty system seemed to only be temporary solutions to the emu problem.

As in 1934, 1943, and 1948 farmers again requested military aid but these times their Government refused.

In the end, someone had the idea to put up fencing to stop the emus gaining access to the crops. This was extremely effective.

In 1950, the army did release half a million bullets to farmers to help them deal with the emus.

The combination of fencing and culling of the initial large population of emus, seems to have been effective. Peace between the Australian farmers and emus has existed since.

Best Wishes,

Antony

Royal Navy Fact:

The 'Clacker Mechanics' is a slang term for the chefs onboard ships.

Week 49 - Quiz: Flags of the World
Hi Roy,

This week it's guess the flags. Here are some flags, guess which country they are from:

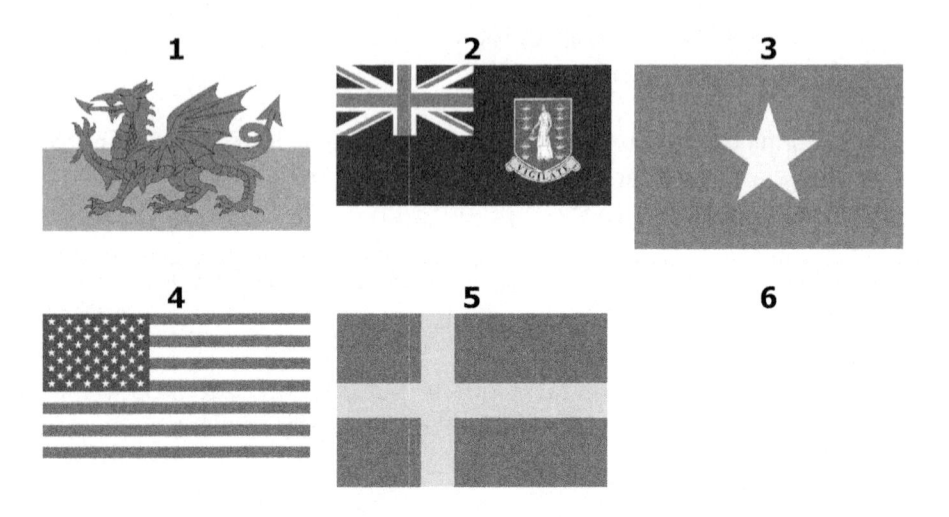

1

2

3

4

5

6

My Royal Navy Friend

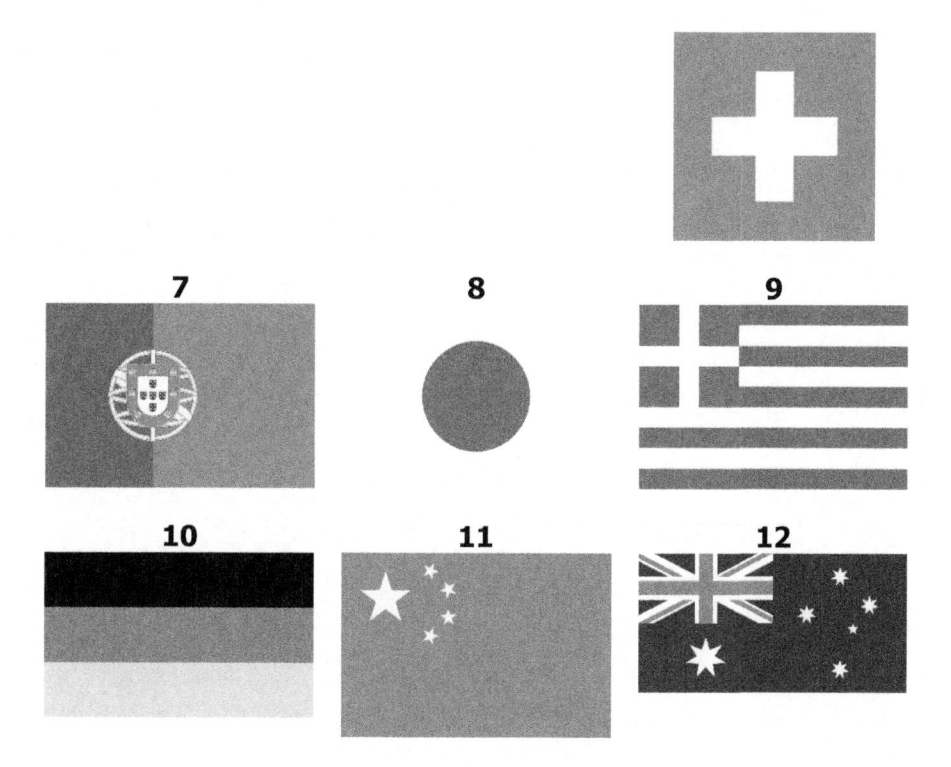

Answers on the next page.
AnswersIda and Louis
1. Wales
2. British Virgin Islands
3. Vietnam
4. United States of America
5. Sweden
6. Switzerland
7. Portugal
8. Japan
9. Greece
10. Germany
11. China
12. Australia

Write Soon,

Antony

> Royal Navy Fact:
>
> In 2022, there were 17 deaths for Royal Navy personnel. This was lower than any other branch of the Armed Forces.

Week 50 - Legendary Characters from the UK
Ahoy Sailor,

We have many legendary characters in the UK. A legend is a story about a person from history, which made a significant impact on the people. Over time, the story is retold to the next generation, verbally, in writing, on the radio, or on TV/film screens. Usually the story has elements of truth, but gets embellished.

Robin Hood
The story goes that Robin Hood stole from the rich to give to the poor in Nottingham. He is said to have lived in Sherwood Forest, worn green attire and been a good Archer. He had a band of merry men and Marrian, a woman whom he loved.

It's hard to separate fact from fiction. But most historians agree the story must have been based on a real person originally.

King Arther & his Knights of the Round Table
King Arther, his knights of the round table, Camelot, the quest for the Holy Grail, the Lancelot/Guinever romance, Excalibur, Merlin, Lady of the Lake, there's so many elements to this story that's been told countless times.

Again it's hard to separate fact and fiction, but historians agree that King Arther must have been originally based on a real person.

Merlin
Merlin was a Wizard, a Wizeman and Advisor to King Arther. He is thought of as an older gentleman with a long white beard. Merlin is said to have been intelligent, cunning and gifted with magical powers. He is usually perceived as on the side of good, although some do question his motives and intentions. Merlin is a very popular character in folklore.

An image of the Green Man, taken at Tynemouth Priory in 2018.

The Green Man
The Green Man is a legend that has its origins in Paganism. Paganism was the main religion in the UK prior to Christianity.

The Green Man is depicted as having a green face with holly and oak leafs on it. He comes from Mother Nature. The story shows the Green Man in different stages of his life over 1 year and symbolises rebirth.

Very early Christian churches, priories and abbeys were built by pagans who had recently converted to Christianity. That is why you can often find green men integrated into the architecture of these buildings (see left).

Lady Godiva

Historical records clearly demonstrate that Lady Godiva was a real woman. But what is legendary fiction is her famous naked ride through Coventry in protest of oppressive taxation. Some scholars believe the naked horse ride never happened.

Best Wishes,

Antony

Royal Navy Fact:

It takes 32 weeks to train to join the Royal Marines. The last week of training, recruits have to complete a series of tests. These tests test recruits' physical and mental endurance.

Week 51 - A Survival Guide to a Zombie Apocalypse
Hello Roy,

You've nearly done a whole year in the Royal Navy already, where did that go?

Apart from dinosaurs, you know I also love a good zombie film. We've all thought about how we'd survive a zombie apocalypse. Here is my brief guide to surviving a zombie apocalypse:

1. **Choose Your Weapon -** Cricket bats, golf clubs, that sort of thing. In America obviously you'd use guns, but we don't really have that option in the UK. The good thing about cricket bats and golf clubs is that they can't run out of bullets.

2. **Save People (with skills)** - I'm going to sound harsh here. But save people with essential skills you'll need for survival. So people like Doctors, Nurses, Farmers, Police Officers, Soldiers, Teachers, etc.

3. **Find Your Food** - Find the food you need for the immediate survival of your group. Think about the medium to long term as well. Food that is ambient (can be stored at room temperature without going off) and food with long expiry dates (think tinned food) are good to get a stash of.

4. **Get a Mode of Transport** - Getting a decent mode of transport will be essential to the survival of your group. Remember that zombies don't know the rules of road safety, and even if they did it's unlikely that they'd comply. So make sure that any mode of transport can take out a zombie without having to stop.

5. **Raid a Pharmacy** - Basic medications, like antibiotics can save lives. So make sure you raid a pharmacy and stock up.

6. **Travel to Your New Home** - Choose your new home wisely. It should be defensible against zombies, but also against other people. The unsavoury kind.

7. **Find a Source of Freshwater** - In the short term bottled water and bottled drinks are fine. But for long term survival your group is going to need a source of freshwater. There may also be fish in the freshwater that your group can eat. So doublewin.

8. **Fortify Your Home** - Extra fortification is always better than not having enough. Safety is survival.

9. **Relax & Ensure Plenty of Leisure Activities** - Your group can then relax, safe and secure. Ensure there are plenty of leisure activities to keep members of your group entertained. Remember that at least initially you're unlikely to have electricity. So a good supply of board games and books are essential.

Best Wishes,

Antony

> Royal Navy Fact:
>
> Being a spouse of someone in the Royal Navy can be difficult at times. As well as not seeing your partner for months, there's always a risk that they could be killed in the line of duty. In addition, if you live with them you may have to move if their deployment changes.
>
> For those with children, the spouses often report that it feels like they are single parents. Raising their children on their own without the support of their Royal Navy partner.

Week 52 - Ida & Louise Cook: An Extraordinary & Inspirational Story

Hi Roy,

My last email. A whole year in the Royal Navy. Well done, I'm so proud of you.

There's nothing more inspiring to me than ordinary people that do the extraordinary for others. The story of Ida and Louise Cook is one such story.

Ida and Louise were British sisters who worked as Clerks for the Civil Service. Ida also wrote romance books under the pen name Mary Burchell, authoring a staggering 112 books in her writing career.

These sisters loved the Opera and would often travel abroad together to see their favourite singers and performances.

Sometime in the 1930s they began hearing about how bad Jewish people were being treated in Germany and Austria.

The sisters travelled to both of these countries under the guise

Ida & Louise Cook (Image from Holocaust Memorial Day Trust, 2019)

of seeing Operas and witnessing this poor treatment of the Jews for themselves. Then something remarkable and extraordinary happened: These two incredible and amazing ladies decided that they must help as many Jewish people as they could to escape this persecution.

Ida and Louise could see that it was only going to get worse for Jewish people in Germany and Austria. Remember this was before the outbreak of World War 2, before the concentration camps and genocide that would follow.

Jews were free to leave Germany and Austria at the time, but they weren't allowed to take any assets with them. This meant no money and no valuables. The policy of the UK and many other countries that were safe for Jewish people was that they had to prove they had the financial assets to support themselves and their families.

This meant the Jewish people were essentially stuck in Germany and Austria. Now at this point in the story, I want to scream: *What were the UK Government and Governments of safe countries thinking with this ridiculous policy? Why weren't the general population outraged by this policy?*

But what we have to remember is that at the time, there was no internet or social media. Many people didn't travel abroad. People weren't as connected as they are now. So the vast majority of the general public didn't know what Jewish people were experiencing in Germany and Austria.

Back to the story. Ida and Louise came up with a plan. They would travel to Germany and Austria as often as they could, using the guise of going to see the Opera as the reason for their frequent travels. On the return journey they would smuggle anything of value given to them by Jewish families. This was so that Jewish families could prove to the UK Government that financially they could support themselves.

Ida and Louise's plan not only took a great deal of planning, their own money and time, but came at a huge personal risk. Imagine if they had been discovered in Germany and Austria.

In November 1938, just less than a year before World War 2 officially started, in the dark of night the Jewish people were targeted in Germany and Austria.

Over two nights, Jewish homes and businesses were destroyed, Synagogues (Jewish places of worship) were attacked and there are even reports of individual Jewish people being arrested without cause. This was all backed by the Germany and Austria Governments and citizens were actively encouraged to participate in the assaults on the Jewish communities.

Ida and Louise's response was fantastic. It was to up their game. They continued the asset smuggling, but went further. Ida and Louise worked hard in the UK to make sure officials signed off as many visas as possible, as quickly as possible, to save as many Jews as possible.

Ida travelled throughout England, making as many people aware of the situation for Jewish people in Germany and Austria as she could. In some of these talks she also raised small amounts of money for Jewish people that needed help. Every penny went to the Jewish people in need.

Ida and Louise rented a flat in London for homeless Jewish people to live whilst they established a life in the UK. The cost of this flat being paid by Ida and Louise.

Ida and Louise took no payment for their work from the Jewish people. They paid for everything themselves, mostly funding their endeavours through Ida's fiction writing.

In total, Ida and Louise saved 29 Jewish people. They helped them escape persecution and come to the safety of the UK. Throughout their lives Ida and Louise kept in touch with these people, keeping an active interest in their lives and continuing to support them in any way that they could.

What an incredible true story of two wonderfully kind, compassionate and inspirational people.

Best Wishes,

Antony

Afterword
Dear Reader,

In the introduction to this book, I said that it was about wanting to maintain a relationship with my dear friend Roy. That is true.

But what also is true, is that the idea was partly inspired by letters wives wrote to their husbands in World War 2. These letters have been turned into radio plays, TV shows and even films.

The title of this book was originally *Emails to My Royal Navy Friend*, but later shortened to *My Royal Navy Friend.*

As anyone that has ever created anything will tell you, when you put a creative work out into the world you never know what reactions to the work you're going to get. This is probably the biggest source of anxiety for any creator.

What I hope comes across clearly in this book is my deep respect for all Armed Service personnel and their families. They do an incredible job, often in difficult circumstances without complaint or without receiving the recognition they deserve.

It takes a special sort of person to serve in the Royal Navy or other Armed Forces. They are required to have integrity, discipline and a strategic mind. Not everyone could do it. I know for me, I certainly couldn't.

So I'll leave you with my heartfelt thanks for the work you do. Most of which, I'll never even know about.

Thank You. My Best Wishes, Now and Forever,

Antony

Printed in Great Britain
by Amazon